This Book Belongs To:

· ·

Christmas 2012

2012 Christmas

with Southern Living®

2012

Christmas

with
Southern Living®

Oxmoor House®

ISBN-13: 978-0-8487-3654-5
ISBN-10: 0-8487-3654-0
ISSN: 0747-7791
Printed in the United States of America
First Printing 2012

Oxmoor House
VP, Publishing Director: Jim Childs
Creative Director: Felicity Keane
Senior Brand Manager: Daniel Fagan
Senior Editor: Rebecca Brennan
Managing Editor: Rebecca Benton

Christmas with Southern Living 2012

Editor: Ashley T. Strickland
Project Editor: Allyson Angle
Director, Test Kitchen: Elizabeth Tyler Austin
Assistant Directors, Test Kitchen: Julie Christopher, Julie Gunter
Test Kitchen Professionals: Wendy Ball, R.D.; Victoria E. Cox; Margaret Monroe Dickey; Stefanie Maloney; Callie Nash; Catherine Crowell Steele; Leah Van Deren
Recipe Editor: Alyson Moreland Haynes
Photography Director: Jim Bathie
Senior Photo Stylist: Kay E. Clarke
Photo Stylist: Katherine Eckert Coyne
Assistant Photo Stylist: Mary Louise Menendez
Senior Production Manager: Greg A. Amason

Contributors
Designer: Carol Damsky
Copy Editor: Donna Baldone
Proofreaders: Adrienne Davis, Polly Linthicum
Indexer: Mary Ann Laurens
Interns: Erin Bishop; Maribeth Browning; Mackenzie Cogle; Jessica Cox, R.D.; Laura Hoxworth; Alicia Lavender; Anna Pollock; Ashley White
Photographers: Brian Francis, Mary Britton Senseney, Becky Luigart-Stayner

Southern Living
Editor: M. Lindsay Bierman
Executive Editors: Rachel Hardage Barrett, Jessica S. Thuston
Food Director: Shannon Sliter Satterwhite
Test Kitchen Director: Rebecca Kracke Gordon
Senior Writer: Donna Florio
Senior Food Editor: Mary Allen Perry
Recipe Editor: JoAnn Weatherly
Assistant Recipe Editor: Ashley Arthur
Test Kitchen Specialist/Food Styling: Vanessa McNeil Rocchio
Test Kitchen Professionals: Norman King, Pam Lolley, Angela Sellers
Homes Editor: Jennifer Kopf
Decorating Editor: Lindsey Ellis Beatty
Director, Editorial Licensing: Katie Terrell Morrow
Assistant Homes Editor: Zoë Gowen
Travel Editors: James T. Black, Kim Cross
Features Editor: Jennifer V. Cole
Senior Photographers: Ralph Anderson, Gary Clark, Art Meripol
Photographer: Robbie Caponetto
Photo Research Coordinator: Ginny P. Allen
Senior Photo Stylist: Buffy Hargett
Editorial Assistants: Cory Bordonaro, Marion Cooper, Stephanie Granada, Pat York

Time Home Entertainment Inc.
Publisher: Richard Fraiman
VP, Strategy & Business Development: Steven Sandonato
Executive Director, Marketing Services: Carol Pittard
Executive Director, Retail & Special Sales: Tom Mifsud
Director, Bookazine Development & Marketing: Laura Adam
Publishing Director: Joy Butts
Finance Director: Glenn Buonocore
Associate General Counsel: Helen Wan

Cover: Turtle Brownie Torte (page 144)

Back Cover: Outdoor Holiday Wreath (page 54)
Herb- and Citrus-Glazed Turkey (page 29)
Spice Candles (page 155)

Welcome

Christmas is a magical time of year, and this year's edition of
Christmas with Southern Living is filled with holiday wonder to make your season bright.
Whether you're looking for a spectacular menu for your Christmas Day feast, a cozy meal
for a chilly winter evening, a special homemade gift from your kitchen, or an easy dish for
a get-together, you'll find the perfect recipes for every occasion in this treasured collection
of over 100 test-kitchen–approved recipes.

We've also gathered our favorite ideas for festive decorating. From merry mantels and a
perfectly trimmed tree to whimsical children's rooms, we've got you covered when it comes
to making your home sparkle for the season. Still trying to cross off everyone on your Christmas
gift list? Take a look at our special gift giving section where you'll find canned goodies as well as
homemade decorations.

We hope this edition brings joy to your holidays. Thanks for allowing us to celebrate with you.

Wishing you a wonderful holiday season,

Ashley T. Strickland
Editor

CONTENTS

Entertain

Gather family and friends around your holiday
table to enjoy these delicious menus that
celebrate the season.

Hearty HOMESTYLE BREAKFAST

RISE AND SHINE TO THIS COMFORTING
BREAKFAST FIT FOR SANTA AND
ALL OF HIS ELVES.

MENU

Sparkling Cranberry Cider

Old Bay Bloody Mary

Tropical Bananas Foster Waffles

Savory Breakfast Sausage

Honey-Rosemary Broiled
Grapefruit

Serves 10 to 12

Sparkling Cranberry Cider
Tropical Bananas Foster Waffles
Savory Breakfast Sausage

Sparkling Cranberry Cider

(pictured on page 10)
Makes: 8 to 10 servings • Hands-On Time: 7 min. • Total Time: 37 min.

Be sure to add the sparkling cider just before serving so that it doesn't lose its fizz.

½ tsp. ground ginger
½ tsp. orange zest
¼ tsp. ground cloves
1 (12-oz.) can frozen cranberry juice cocktail
1 (3-inch) cinnamon stick
2 (750-milliliter) bottles sparkling apple cider, chilled

1. Place first 5 ingredients in a small saucepan. Bring to a boil over medium-high heat, stirring until cranberry juice cocktail melts. Remove from heat; let cool 30 minutes.
2. Pour cranberry juice mixture into a pitcher. Add cider, and stir gently. Serve over ice. Serve immediately.

Old Bay Bloody Mary

Makes: 6 to 8 servings • Hands-On Time: 8 min. • Total Time: 8 min.

Not your standard Bloody Mary, this one derives its kick from Old Bay seasoning, concocted with 18 spices and herbs, and fresh horseradish. Have a variety of hot sauces on hand for Bloody Mary connoisseurs who like to turn up the heat.

½ cup beef broth
¼ cup fresh lime juice
¼ cup Worcestershire sauce
2 Tbsp. refrigerated horseradish
1 tsp. Old Bay seasoning
½ tsp. salt
¾ tsp. freshly ground pepper
1 (46-oz.) bottle tomato juice, chilled
Hot sauce to taste
2½ cups vodka
Garnishes: lime wedges, celery ribs with leaves, spicy pickled asparagus, spicy pickled okra, large pimiento-stuffed Spanish olives, extra-large cooked peeled shrimp with tails intact

1. Stir together first 9 ingredients in a large pitcher. Cover and chill.
2. Stir in vodka. Serve over ice. Garnish, if desired.

Old Bay Bloody Mary

Tropical Bananas Foster Waffles

(pictured on page 10)
Makes: 10 servings • Hands-On Time: 12 min. • Total Time: 42 min.

Everyone will love this Southern twist to the iconic Belgian waffle served with strawberries and chocolate sauce.

- 1 (¼-oz.) envelope active dry yeast
- ¼ cup warm water (100° to 110°)
- 2½ cups all-purpose flour
- 1 Tbsp. sugar
- ½ tsp. baking soda
- ½ tsp. salt
- 4 egg yolks
- 1¾ cups buttermilk
- ⅓ cup butter, melted
- 1 tsp. vanilla extract
- 4 egg whites
- Caramelized Bananas
- Sweetened whipped cream
- ⅓ cup coconut, toasted
- ⅓ cup candied pecans or toasted macadamia nuts

1. Combine yeast and warm water in a 1-cup glass measuring cup; let stand 5 minutes.
2. Meanwhile, combine flour and next 3 ingredients in a large bowl; make a well in center of mixture. Whisk together egg yolks, buttermilk, and next 2 ingredients. Whisk in yeast mixture; add to dry mixture, stirring just until moistened.
3. Beat egg whites at high speed with an electric mixer until stiff peaks form. Fold beaten egg white into batter. Cook in a preheated, oiled waffle iron until done.
4. Meanwhile, prepare Caramelized Bananas.
5. Dollop whipped cream onto waffles. Top with Caramelized Bananas, and sprinkle with coconut and nuts.

Caramelized Bananas

Makes: 10 servings • Hands-On Time: 3 min. • Total Time: 10 min.

- 3 medium-size ripe bananas
- ½ cup butter
- ¾ cup firmly packed light brown sugar
- 1 Tbsp. corn syrup
- ⅓ cup evaporated milk
- 1 tsp. vanilla extract
- 2 Tbsp. dark rum (optional)

1. Cut bananas in half crosswise; cut halves in half lengthwise.
2. Melt butter in a large skillet; stir in brown sugar and corn syrup. Bring to a boil over medium heat; stir in milk. Cook, stirring constantly, 1 minute. Remove from heat. Stir in vanilla and, if desired, rum. Add bananas, stirring just until bananas begin to soften. Remove from heat. Serve immediately.

Savory Breakfast Sausage

Makes: 12 servings • Hands-On Time: 15 min. • Total Time: 9 hr., 35 min.

Fresh herbs combined with ground pork make a perfect savory complement to a "sweet" breakfast lineup.

- 3 lb. ground pork
- 3 Tbsp. finely chopped fresh sage
- 4 tsp. chopped fresh thyme
- 1 Tbsp. kosher salt
- 1 Tbsp. light brown sugar
- 2 tsp. freshly ground black pepper
- 1½ tsp. minced fresh rosemary
- 1 tsp. dry mustard
- ½ tsp. ground red pepper
- 1 Tbsp. canola oil

1. Combine first 9 ingredients in a large bowl. Shape mixture into 24 (½-inch-thick) patties. Cover and chill at least 8 hours.
2. Heat oil in a large skillet over medium-high heat. Cook patties in oil, in 3 batches, 3 to 4 minutes on each side or until done.

Honey-Rosemary Broiled Grapefruit

Makes: 12 servings • Hands-On Time: 9 min. • Total Time: 1 hr.

Celebrate seasonal citrus with grapefruit drizzled with a rosemary-honey syrup.

½   cup sugar
1½ Tbsp. Tupelo or other honey
2   (3-inch) sprigs fresh rosemary
6   ruby red grapefruit, halved
6   Tbsp. turbinado sugar

1. Combine first 3 ingredients and ¼ cup water in a medium saucepan. Bring to a boil; boil 5 minutes. Let cool completely. Remove and discard rosemary.
2. Preheat broiler. Place grapefruit halves on a large foil-lined jelly-roll pan. Brush syrup generously over tops of grapefruit; sprinkle top of each grapefruit with 1½ tsp. turbinado sugar. Broil 6 inches from heat 7 minutes or until sugar melts and begins to caramelize. Brush grapefruit with pan juices. Serve immediately.

Note: For a more intense rosemary flavor, prepare syrup 1 day ahead. Do not remove rosemary sprig until just before brushing syrup on grapefruit.

After-Santa
SIT-DOWN

ENJOY THIS CASUAL LUNCH AFTER A
MORNING FILLED WITH OPENING GIFTS
FROM SANTA.

MENU

Cold Roasted Tenderloin of Beef
with Creamy Horseradish Sauce

Marinated Roasted Red Peppers

Rosemary-Gruyère Buns

Asian Pear and Hazelnut Salad

Malt Vinegar Potato Wedges

Sachertorte

Serves 8

GAME PLAN

2 days before:
- Prepare cake layer, and split; wrap airtightly and freeze.

1 day before:
- Prepare horseradish sauce; cover and chill.
- Prepare beef; cover and chill overnight.
- Prepare marinated peppers; cover and chill overnight.
- Prepare apricot filling for cake; cover and chill.

3 hours before:
- Prepare buns up to baking step.
- Thaw cake layers.

2 hours before:
- Prepare glaze, and assemble cake.
- Prepare dressing, and assemble salad separately, omitting pears; cover and chill.

1 hour before:
- Prepare potatoes; keep warm.
- Slice beef.

30 minutes before:
- Bake rolls.
- Prepare whipped cream for cake.

Just before:
- Slice pears, and toss salad.
- Garnish cake.

EDITOR'S FAVORITE   MAKE AHEAD

Cold Roasted Tenderloin of Beef with Creamy Horseradish Sauce

Makes: 10 to 12 servings • Hands-On Time: 25 min. • Total Time: 2 hr., 10 min., plus overnight to chill

Juicy herbed beef tenderloin tastes delicious when accompanied by Creamy Horseradish Sauce. English cucumber adds an unexpected crunch to the sauce. Have a small bowl of horseradish available for guests who enjoy an extra hit of pungent heat.

2 Tbsp. chopped fresh rosemary
2 Tbsp. chopped fresh thyme
1 Tbsp. kosher salt
1 Tbsp. freshly ground pepper
3 Tbsp. olive oil
6 garlic cloves, minced
4¾- to 5-lb. trimmed and tied beef tenderloin
Creamy Horseradish Sauce
Garnish: fresh rosemary sprigs

1. Preheat oven to 500°. Combine first 6 ingredients in a small bowl; rub mixture over beef. Place beef in a large roasting pan.
2. Bake at 500° for 10 minutes. Reduce oven temperature to 350°. Bake for 30 more minutes or until a meat thermometer registers 140° or until desired degree of doneness. Remove from oven, and cool until room temperature (1 hour).
3. Meanwhile, prepare Creamy Horseradish Sauce.
4. Wrap beef in plastic wrap; chill overnight. Cut roast into ½-inch slices; arrange slices on a serving platter. Garnish, if desired. Serve with Creamy Horseradish Sauce.

QUICK & EASY
Creamy Horseradish Sauce

Makes: 3 cups • Hands-On Time: 5 min. • Total Time: 5 min.

⅔ cup refrigerated horseradish
½ cup finely chopped English cucumber
½ tsp. salt
1 (16-oz.) container sour cream

1. Stir together all ingredients in a medium bowl; chill.

Marinated Roasted Red Peppers

Makes: 8 to 10 servings • Hands-On Time: 12 min. • Total Time: 30 min., plus 1 day for marinating

Use a mix of red, yellow, and orange bell peppers for added color.

4 large red bell peppers
⅓ cup extra virgin olive oil
3 Tbsp. balsamic vinegar
1 Tbsp. Dijon mustard
1 Tbsp. honey
½ tsp. salt
¼ tsp. freshly ground pepper
¾ cup thinly sliced sweet onion (about ½ medium)
¼ cup chopped green onions
2 garlic cloves, crushed
1 rosemary sprig

1. Preheat broiler. Quarter peppers lengthwise; remove seeds and membranes. Place bell pepper, skin side up, on an aluminum foil-lined baking sheet. Broil 5 inches from heat 8 to 10 minutes or until bell pepper looks blistered. Place bell pepper in a large zip-top plastic freezer bag; seal bag. Let stand 10 minutes to loosen skins. Remove bell pepper from bag, reserving bag. Peel bell pepper; cut into ½-inch-thick slices.
2. Place oil and next 5 ingredients in reserved bag. Seal bag; shake to blend. Add roasted bell pepper, onion, and next 3 ingredients; seal bag, and shake to coat vegetables. Chill up to 24 hours, turning bag occasionally. Remove and discard rosemary sprig before serving.

Rosemary-Gruyère Buns

Marinated Roasted Red Peppers

Cold Roasted Tenderloin of Beef with Creamy Horseradish Sauce

Rosemary-Gruyère Buns

Makes: 1½ dozen • Hands-On Time: 30 min. • Total Time: 2 hr., 30 min.

These ultimate savory yeast rolls—bedecked with crispy cheese and studded with flavorful chopped rosemary—are the perfect companions for tender roast beef.

- 1½ cups milk
- ½ cup butter, divided
- ¼ cup warm water (100° to 110°)
- 1 Tbsp. sugar
- 1 (¼-oz.) package active dry yeast
- 1 Tbsp. chopped fresh rosemary
- 2 tsp. salt
- 1 tsp. freshly ground pepper
- 2 large eggs
- 2½ cups (10 oz.) shredded Gruyère cheese, divided
- 5 to 5½ cups all-purpose flour
- 1 large egg, beaten

1. Cook milk and ¼ cup butter in a saucepan over medium-low heat 3 to 5 minutes or until butter melts, stirring occasionally. Let cool to 115°.

2. Meanwhile, combine warm water and next 2 ingredients in a 1-cup liquid measuring cup; let stand 5 minutes.

3. Beat milk mixture, rosemary, salt, pepper, and 2 eggs at medium speed with a heavy-duty electric stand mixer until blended. Beat in 2 cups cheese and yeast mixture. Gradually beat in 5 cups flour. Beat at medium speed 3 minutes.

4. Turn dough out onto a floured surface, and knead until smooth and elastic (about 5 minutes), adding remaining ½ cup flour as necessary to prevent sticking. Place dough in a well-greased bowl, turning to grease top. Cover and let rise in a warm place (85°), free from drafts, about 1 hour, or until doubled in bulk.

5. Punch dough down; turn out onto a lightly floured surface, and knead 2 or 3 times. Divide dough into 18 equal portions. Shape each portion into a 2½-inch oval. Place rolls 1½ inches apart on lightly greased baking sheets. Cover and let rise in a warm place (85°), free from drafts, 45 minutes or until doubled in bulk.

6. Preheat oven to 400°. Brush beaten egg over tops of rolls; sprinkle with remaining ½ cup cheese. Bake at 400° for 15 minutes or until golden brown.

7. Melt remaining ¼ cup butter; brush over rolls.

Asian Pear and Hazelnut Salad

Makes: 8 to 10 servings • Hands-On Time: 10 min. • Total Time: 10 min.

Winter fruits Asian pear and pomegranate and rich, fragrant hazelnuts are tossed together with baby greens and a slightly sweet, nutty vinaigrette in this healthy yet satisfying salad.

- 3 Tbsp. rice vinegar
- 2 Tbsp. fresh orange juice
- 1 Tbsp. honey
- ½ tsp. kosher salt
- ⅛ tsp. freshly ground pepper
- ⅓ cup hazelnut oil
- 2 (5-oz.) packages spring greens mix
- ½ cup coarsely chopped hazelnuts, toasted
- ⅓ cup fresh pomegranate seeds
- ¼ cup (1-inch) pieces fresh chives
- 2 Asian pears, cored and sliced

1. Whisk together first 5 ingredients. Slowly whisk in oil.
2. Place greens in a large bowl. Add hazelnuts and remaining ingredients. Drizzle with vinaigrette, and toss gently.

PEAR PRIMER

Asian pears, also known as apple pears, make an appearance in early fall. Their crisp, crunchy texture, subtle sweetness, and juiciness make them ideal for this holiday salad. Look for pears that are firm to the touch. If you are unable to find Asian pears, Bosc or Bartlett pears make a nice substitute.

Malt Vinegar Potato Wedges

Makes: 8 servings • Hands-On Time: 7 min. • Total Time: 52 min.

Malt vinegar–flavored sea salt provides a tangy flavor component to these crisp-on-the-outside, fluffy-on-the-inside potatoes.

- 6 Tbsp. olive oil
- 2 Tbsp. coarse ground mustard seed
- 2 Tbsp. chopped fresh rosemary
- 2 Tbsp. malt vinegar–flavored sea salt, divided
- 8 baking potatoes (about 5 lbs.), each cut lengthwise into 16 wedges

1. Preheat oven to 450°. Line 2 large baking sheets with aluminum foil; coat foil with cooking spray. Stir together first 3 ingredients and 3 tsp. sea salt in a large bowl. Add potato wedges, tossing to coat. Spread potato mixture in a single layer on prepared baking sheets.

2. Bake at 450° for 45 minutes or until potato is golden brown and tender, stirring potatoes halfway through. Sprinkle with remaining 3 tsp. sea salt.

Note: We tested with Williams-Sonoma ground mustard seed and malt vinegar–flavored sea salt.

Malt Vinegar Potato Wedges

Sachertorte

Makes: 12 servings • Hands-On Time: 25 min. • Total Time: 3 hr., 5 min.

This "grown-up" version of the famous Viennese chocolate cake boasts a dense texture and rich, shiny glaze. The apricot filling and rich cream topping are subtly flavored with orange liqueur.

CAKE
Parchment paper
- ¾ cup butter, softened
- ¾ cup granulated sugar, divided
- 5 large eggs, separated
- 1 tsp. vanilla extract
- 5 oz. bittersweet chocolate, melted and cooled
- ¾ cup all-purpose flour

APRICOT-ORANGE FILLING
- 1 cup apricot preserves
- ¼ cup orange liqueur

GLAZE
- 6 oz. bittersweet chocolate, chopped
- ½ cup whipping cream
- 2 Tbsp. light corn syrup
- 2 Tbsp. butter

GRAND MARNIER CREAM
- 1 cup heavy whipping cream
- 2 Tbsp. powdered sugar
- 1 Tbsp. orange liqueur

REMAINING INGREDIENTS
Garnish: chocolate curls

1. Prepare Cake: Preheat oven to 350°. Line bottom of a 9-inch springform pan with parchment paper; coat pan with cooking spray.

2. Beat ¾ cup butter at medium speed with a heavy-duty electric mixer until creamy (about 2 minutes). Gradually add ½ cup granulated sugar, beating until light and fluffy. Add egg yolks, 1 at a time, beating just until yellow disappears after each addition. Add vanilla and melted chocolate, beating on low speed just until blended. Gradually add flour, beating ust until blended. In a separate bowl, beat egg whites at high speed with an electric mixer until foamy; gradually add remaining ¼ cup granulated sugar, beating until soft peaks form. Fold in one-fourth of egg whites into batter; gently fold in remaining egg white mixture. Pour batter into pan.

3. Bake at 350° for 35 minutes or until a wooden pick inserted in center comes out clean. Cool completely in pan on a wire rack (about 2 hours). Run a knife around edge of cake to loosen; invert onto work surface. Cut horizontally into 3 layers.

4. Prepare Apricot-Orange Filling: Process apricot preserves

Sachertorte

in a food processor 30 seconds or until smooth. Transfer to a small saucepan, and cook over medium-low heat until melted, stirring often. Remove from heat, and stir in ¼ cup liqueur.
5. Brush ½ cup apricot mixture over 1 cake layer; top with second cake layer. Brush with ½ cup apricot mixture; top with remaining cake layer. Brush top with remaining ¼ cup apricot mixture. Set cake on a wire rack over a rimmed baking sheet.
6. Prepare Glaze: Place chopped chocolate in a medium bowl. Combine whipping cream and corn syrup in a small saucepan;

bring to a simmer over medium heat. Pour over chocolate; let stand 1 minute. Whisk until smooth; stir in butter. Pour glaze over cake, covering top and sides completely. Chill cake 1 hour or until glaze is set.
7. Just before serving, prepare Grand Marnier Cream: Beat 1 cup whipping cream with an electric mixer until foamy; add powdered sugar and orange liqueur, beating until soft peaks form. Cut cake into 12 wedges. Top with Grand Marnier Cream. Garnish, if desired.

Herb- and Citrus-Glazed Turkey
Cranberry Clementine Relish
Sweet and Savory Roasted Green Beans
Savory Bread Pudding with Sage, Mushrooms, and Apple

THANKS

GATHER AROUND THE TABLE AND
CELEBRATE THE YEAR'S BLESSINGS WITH
THIS TRADITIONAL HOLIDAY MEAL.

MENU

Grapefruit-Ginger Bourbon Sour

Sparkling Blood Orange Cocktail

Parmesan-Crusted Crab Cake
Bites with Chive Aïoli

Herb- and Citrus-Glazed Turkey

Cranberry Clementine Relish

Sweet and Savory Roasted
Green Beans

Parsnip Purée

Savory Bread Pudding with Sage,
Mushrooms, and Apple

Spicy Smoked Pecans with
Bacon Salt

Southern Cheese Plate

Dulce de Leche–Pumpkin
Cheesecake with Candied
Almonds

Serves 10

GAME PLAN

2 days before:
- Prepare Spicy Smoked Pecans and Candied Almonds; store in airtight container.

1 day before:
- Prepare and bake cheesecake. Cover and chill overnight.
- Prepare syrup for bourbon sours; cover and chill.
- Prepare blood orange cocktail, omitting sparkling water; cover and chill.
- Prepare crab cake mixture; cover and chill.
- Prepare Chive Aïoli; cover and chill.
- Prepare Citrus Compound Butter for turkey; cover and chill.
- Prepare Cranberry Clementine Relish; cover and chill.
- Assemble bread pudding; cover and chill, unbaked.

4 hours before:
- Prepare and bake turkey.
- Assemble cheese plate. Cover and chill.

1 hour before:
- Prepare green beans; keep warm.
- Prepare Parsnip Purée; keep warm.
- Bake bread pudding; keep warm.
- Set out cheese plate.

Just before:
- Stir together blood orange mixture and sparkling water.
- Assemble bourbon sours.
- Slice turkey.
- Garnish cheesecake.

Grapefruit-Ginger Bourbon Sour

Makes: 6 servings • Hands-On Time: 5 min. • Total Time: 1 hr., 8 min.

Put a new twist on this favorite mixed drink by using grapefruit and ginger in a homemade sour mix.

- 1 cup superfine sugar
- 1 (3-inch) piece fresh ginger, peeled and thinly sliced
- 1¾ cups fresh grapefruit juice (about 2 grapefruit)
- ½ cup fresh lime juice (about 3 large)
- 2 cups bourbon

1. Stir together 1 cup water, sugar, and ginger in a 2-cup glass measuring cup. Microwave at HIGH 3 minutes or until boiling. Stir until sugar dissolves; let cool completely (about 1 hour).
2. Remove and discard ginger from syrup. Stir together syrup and juices.
3. Fill 6 double old-fashioned glasses with crushed ice. Add ½ cup juice mixture and ⅓ cup bourbon to each glass; stir. Serve immediately.

QUICK & EASY
Sparkling Blood Orange Cocktail

Makes: 6 servings • Hands-On Time: 5 min. • Total Time: 5 min.

Blood oranges come into season just in time for the winter holidays, their crimson flesh producing a sweet juice with festive color. Paired with fresh lime for bright acidity and good-quality tequila, this drink is a great way to spin a new start on the holiday festivities.

- 1½ cups fresh blood orange juice
- 1 cup white tequila
- ½ cup red vermouth
- ¼ cup agave nectar
- 2 Tbsp. fresh lime juice
- ¾ cup sparkling water
- Garnish: blood orange wedges

1. Stir together first 5 ingredients in a pitcher. Chill until ready to serve.
2. Fill 6 highball glasses with ice. Pour about ½ cup blood orange mixture into each glass. Fill each glass with 2 Tbsp. sparkling water; stir. Garnish, if desired. Serve immediately.

Grapefruit-Ginger
Bourbon Sour

Parmesan-Crusted Crab Cake Bites with Chive Aïoli

Makes: 12 servings • Hands-On Time: 18 min. • Total Time: 48 min.

These miniature crab cakes are baked rather than panfried and are easy to prepare for a crowd. Use a 1-inch scoop to portion the crab mixture evenly among the mini muffin cups. The crab mixture can be made a day in advance. Cover and store in the refrigerator.

      6 oz. fresh lump crabmeat, drained
      2 (3-oz.) packages cream cheese, softened
    ⅔ cup grated Parmesan cheese, divided
      3 Tbsp. mayonnaise
      2 tsp. Dijon mustard
      1 tsp. Worcestershire sauce
    ¾ tsp. Old Bay seasoning
    ½ tsp. lemon zest
      1 egg yolk
   1½ Tbsp. chopped fresh parsley
   1¼ cups Japanese breadcrumbs (panko)
    ¼ cup butter, melted
         Chive Aïoli

1. Preheat oven to 350°. Generously grease 2 (12-cup) miniature muffin pans. Pick crabmeat, removing any bits of shell.

2. Stir cream cheese in a large bowl until smooth. Add ⅓ cup Parmesan cheese and next 6 ingredients; stir until smooth. Fold in crabmeat and parsley.

3. Combine remaining ⅓ cup Parmesan cheese, breadcrumbs, and melted butter in a medium bowl; toss with a fork until breadcrumbs are moistened. Spoon 1 Tbsp. breadcrumb mixture into each muffin cup; press into bottom and up sides to form crust. Spoon 1 Tbsp. crab mixture into each crust.

4. Bake at 350° for 25 minutes or until golden brown. Cool in pans 5 minutes. Run a knife around edges of crab cakes to loosen; gently lift cakes from pan. Serve warm or at room temperature topped with Chive Aïoli.

QUICK & EASY
Chive Aïoli

Makes: ½ cup • Hands-On Time: 4 min. • Total Time: 4 min.

Prepare this aïoli up to 1 day in advance; cover and chill.

    ½ cup mayonnaise
      1 Tbsp. chopped fresh chives
      1 tsp. Dijon mustard
      1 garlic clove, pressed

1. Combine all ingredients in a small bowl. Cover and chill.

Herb- and Citrus-Glazed Turkey

Makes: 8 to 10 servings • Hands-On Time: 23 min. • Total Time: 4 hr., 19 min.

Using a compound butter under the skin and stuffing the turkey with citrus and fresh herbs ensures a flavorful, juicy bird.

CITRUS COMPOUND BUTTER
- ½ cup unsalted butter, softened
- 1 Tbsp. salt
- 2 Tbsp. chopped fresh thyme
- 2 Tbsp. chopped fresh sage
- 1 Tbsp. chopped fresh rosemary
- 1 tsp. freshly ground pepper
- 1 tsp. tangerine zest
- 1 tsp. lime zest
- 1 tsp. Meyer lemon zest
- 3 garlic cloves, minced

TURKEY
- 1 (12-lb.) whole fresh or frozen turkey, thawed
- 1 Tbsp. salt
- 1 tangerine, halved
- 1 Meyer lemon, halved
- 1 lime, halved
- ½ cup celery leaves
- ⅓ cup fresh thyme sprigs
- ¼ cup fresh sage sprigs
- 1½ cups chicken broth

GLAZE
- ½ cup unsalted butter
- ⅓ cup orange marmalade
- 2 Tbsp. honey
- 1 Tbsp. salt
- 2 tsp. Meyer lemon zest
- 1 tsp. lime zest
- 1 tsp. chopped fresh thyme
- 1 tsp. chopped fresh sage

REMAINING INGREDIENTS
- 2 Tbsp. all-purpose flour
- Salt and pepper to taste
- Garnishes: clementines, Meyer lemons, pecans, kumquats

1. Prepare Citrus Compound Butter: Stir together all ingredients in a medium bowl until blended.

2. Prepare Turkey: Preheat oven to 325°. Remove giblets and neck, and rinse turkey with cold water. Drain cavity well; pat dry. Loosen and lift skin from turkey with fingers, without totally detaching skin; spread compound butter underneath. Carefully replace skin. Sprinkle cavity with 1 Tbsp. salt. Squeeze citrus halves into cavity; place squeezed fruit, celery leaves, and next 2 ingredients in cavity. Tie ends of legs together with string; tuck wingtips under. Place turkey on a roasting rack in an aluminum foil–lined roasting pan, breast side up. Pour broth in bottom of roasting pan.

3. Prepare Glaze: Place ½ cup unsalted butter, marmalade, and honey in a small saucepan. Cook over medium-low heat until butter melts. Remove from heat; stir in salt and next 4 ingredients. Brush half of glaze over turkey. Loosely cover turkey with foil.

4. Bake at 325° on lowest oven rack for 1 hour and 30 minutes. Uncover and brush with glaze. Bake 1 hour and 25 more minutes or until a meat thermometer inserted into thickest portion of thigh registers 165°, basting with remaining glaze every 30 minutes. Shield with aluminum foil to prevent excessive browning, if necessary. Remove turkey from oven. Let stand, covered with foil, 30 minutes.

5. Place turkey on a serving platter, reserving drippings in pan. Pour about 1 cup pan drippings into 1-cup glass measuring cup. Let stand 10 minutes, and skim fat from drippings, reserving 1 Tbsp. fat. Heat reserved 1 Tbsp. fat in a small saucepan over medium heat; whisk in flour. Cook 1 minute. Gradually add 1 cup reserved drippings, whisking constantly. Cook 5 minutes or until thickened. Add salt and pepper to taste. Garnish turkey, if desired, and serve with gravy.

MAKE AHEAD
Cranberry Clementine Relish

Makes: 4 cups • Hands-On Time: 10 min. • Total Time: 8 hr., 10 min.

The cranberries in this recipe are left raw and shredded for extra crunch and tartness. Be sure to use clementines which, unlike tangerines, are seedless.

- 4 clementines
- 1 Granny Smith apple, peeled, cored, and cut into eighths
- 1 (12-oz.) package fresh or frozen cranberries, thawed
- ½ cup sugar
- ½ cup honey
- ¼ cup orange liqueur

1. Grate zest from clementines to equal 4 tsp. Peel clementines, and separate into segments. Process zest, clementine segments, apple, and cranberries in a food processor until chopped. Transfer fruit to a bowl. Stir in sugar and next 2 ingredients. Cover and chill overnight. Serve with a slotted spoon.

Sweet and Savory Roasted Green Beans

Makes: 10 to 12 servings • Hands-On Time: 43 min. • Total Time: 43 min.

In this dish, fresh green beans are roasted to bring out their natural sweetness, then combined with savory bacon for added richness and orange zest for a burst of citrus on the palate.

- 3 lb. fresh green beans, trimmed
- 1 Tbsp. olive oil, divided
- 1 tsp. salt
- ¼ tsp. freshly ground pepper
- 6 thick hickory-smoked bacon slices, cut into ½-inch pieces
- 4 large shallots, cut into wedges
- 3 Tbsp. white balsamic vinegar
- 1 Tbsp. honey
- 1 tsp. fresh thyme leaves
- 1 tsp. orange zest
- ⅓ cup chopped hazelnuts, toasted

1. Preheat oven to 425°. Place green beans in a large bowl. Drizzle with olive oil; sprinkle with salt and pepper, tossing to coat. Divide green beans between 2 (15- x 10-inch) jelly-roll pans. Bake at 425° for 25 minutes. Stir and bake 10 more minutes or until tender.

2. Meanwhile, cook bacon in a large skillet over medium-high heat 8 to 10 minutes or until crisp; remove bacon, and drain on paper towels, reserving 2 Tbsp. drippings in skillet. Crumble bacon. Sauté shallots in hot drippings until tender. Add vinegar, stirring to loosen particles from bottom of skillet. Stir in honey.

3. Pour shallot mixture over green beans, and sprinkle with thyme, orange zest, hazelnuts, and bacon. Toss well.

Parsnip Purée

Makes: 10 to 12 servings • Hands-On Time: 15 min. • Total Time: 50 min.

Buttery parsnips are a perfect accompaniment to a holiday meal. Sweeter in flavor than carrots, this side dish is sure to please your guests. Like potatoes, parsnips quickly turn brown when exposed to air, so place in water straight away to avoid oxidation.

- 4 lb. parsnips, peeled and cut into ½-inch slices
- ½ cup butter
- ½ cup chicken broth
- ½ cup half-and-half
- ¾ tsp. sea salt
- ¼ tsp. freshly ground pepper

1. Cook parsnips in boiling, salted water to cover in a large saucepan 30 minutes or until tender. Drain.

2. Process half each of parsnips, butter, broth, and half-and-half in a food processor until smooth, stopping to scrape down sides as needed. Spoon mixture into a large bowl. Repeat procedure with remaining parsnips, butter, broth, and half-and-half; stir in salt and pepper.

MAKE AHEAD

Savory Bread Pudding with Sage, Mushrooms, and Apple

Makes: 12 servings • Hands-On Time: 25 min. • Total Time: 9 hr., 35 min.

Serve these custards in individual 8-oz. ramekins, and bake at 350° for 25 to 30 minutes.

- 1 (1-lb.) loaf ciabatta bread, cut into 1-inch cubes
- ½ cup butter, divided
- 1½ cups chopped sweet onion
- ¾ cup chopped celery
- 2 Tbsp. chopped fresh sage
- 3 (4-oz.) packages wild mushroom blend
- 3 garlic cloves, minced
- 2 Golden Delicious apples, peeled and chopped
- 2 cups heavy cream
- 2 cups milk
- 5 large eggs
- 1¼ tsp. salt
- ¾ tsp. freshly ground pepper

1. Preheat oven to 375°. Place bread cubes on a large rimmed baking sheet. Melt ¼ cup butter in a large skillet over low heat. Drizzle melted butter over bread cubes; toss to coat. Bake at 375° for 20 minutes or until golden, stirring halfway through. Transfer cubes to a large bowl.

2. Melt 3 Tbsp. butter in skillet over medium-high heat. Add onion and next 4 ingredients to skillet; sauté 12 minutes or until tender. Add mushroom mixture to bread cubes.

3. Melt remaining 1 Tbsp. butter in skillet. Add apple; sauté 4 minutes or until golden. Add apple to bread mixture.

4. Whisk together cream and next 4 ingredients. Pour over bread mixture; toss well. Pour bread mixture into a greased 13- x 9-inch baking dish. Cover and chill at least 8 hours.

5. Preheat oven to 350°. Uncover casserole, and bake at 350° for 1 hour and 10 minutes or until set and lightly browned. Let stand 15 minutes.

Savory Bread Pudding with Sage, Mushrooms, and Apple

Spicy Smoked Pecans with Bacon Salt

Makes: about 5 cups • Hands-On Time: 5 min. • Total Time: 1 hr., 5 min.

Hickory-smoked bacon salt is the key ingredient in this addictive snack. Guests won't be able to keep their hands out of the nut bowl!

- ¼ cup firmly packed light brown sugar
- 2 Tbsp. hickory-flavored bacon salt
- 1½ tsp. crushed chipotle chile
- 1½ tsp. smoked serrano chile powder
- 2 egg whites
- 1 lb. pecan halves
- Parchment paper

1. Preheat oven to 250°. Stir together first 4 ingredients in a small bowl. Whisk egg whites in a large bowl until foamy. Add pecans, tossing to coat. Add spice mixture, tossing to coat.
2. Spread nut mixture in a single layer on a parchment paper–lined baking sheet.
3. Bake at 250° for 1 hour, stirring after 30 minutes. Let cool slightly, and break pecans apart. Cool to room temperature. Store in an airtight container up to 2 weeks.

Note: We tested with J & D's hickory-flavored bacon salt and crushed chipotle chile and smoked serrano chile powder from Williams-Sonoma.

Southern Cheese Plate

Makes: 10 to 12 servings • Hands-On Time: 10 min.

Some of our favorite Southern artisanal cheese producers are showcased here with a selection of their fine cheeses. Included is a sampling of sheep, cow, and goat's milk cheeses and suggestions for wine pairings that enhance the flavor profiles of each.

½ cup chopped walnuts, toasted
1 (11-oz.) log Belle Chèvre goat cheese
1 cup fig preserves
1 lb. Champagne grapes, red grapes, red currants or pears, sliced
Assorted crackers
Wine suggestion: semidry white sparkling wine or Sauvignon Blanc

1. Place chopped walnuts in a shallow dish. Roll goat cheese log in walnuts, pressing gently to coat completely.
2. Arrange log on a serving platter alongside a small bowl of fig preserves, Champagne grapes, and an assortment of crackers.

Variation 1

1 lb. Sweet Grass Dairy Asher Blue cow's milk cheese
2 cups hickory-smoked almonds
1 lb. Medjool dates
Almond crackers or buttery crackers
Wine suggestion: Port or full-bodied red wine (such as Cabernet)

Variation 2

1 lb. Locust Grove La Mancha Reserve sheep's milk cheese
1 (4.2-oz.) container quince fruit paste
1½ cups Marcona almonds
Rosemary crackers
Wine suggestion: Spanish sherry (such as Amontillado) or White Meritage (such as St. Supery Vertu)

Variation 3

1 lb. Sweet Grass Dairy Green Hill (Camembert-style) cow's milk cheese
1 cup peach preserves
2 cups pecans, toasted (about ½ lb.)
Assorted butter crackers
Wine suggestion: Champagne or Vouvray (such as Chenin Blanc)

Note: We tested with Chilton County peach preserves. Also, for more information about artisanal cheese producers in the South, visit *southerncheese.com*.
These featured cheeses can be purchased online at Fromagerie Belle Chèvre, Elkmont, Alabama
bellechevre.com
Locust Grove Farm, Knoxville, Tennessee
locustgrovefarm.net
Sweet Grass Dairy, Thomasville, Georgia
sweetgrassdairy.com

Dulce de Leche–Pumpkin Cheesecake with Candied Almonds

Makes: 12 servings • Hands-On Time: 40 min. • Total Time: 11 hr., 37 min.

Sweet milk caramel, or dulce de leche, takes this decadent cheesecake over the top—be sure to save room for dessert!

CRUST
- 2 (5.3-oz.) packages pure butter shortbread cookies
- ½ cup sliced almonds
- ¼ cup butter, melted

FILLING
- 4 (8-oz.) packages cream cheese, softened
- 1 cup sugar
- ½ cup canned dulce de leche
- 4 large eggs
- 1 (15-oz.) can pumpkin
- 1 tsp. ground ginger
- 1 tsp. ground cinnamon
- ½ tsp. ground cloves

CANDIED ALMONDS
- 1 egg white
- 3 Tbsp. sugar
- ½ tsp. ground cinnamon
- 1½ cups sliced almonds
- Parchment paper

TOPPING
- ¾ cup whipping cream, divided
- 1 Tbsp. powdered sugar
- ½ cup canned dulce de leche

1. Prepare Crust: Preheat oven to 350°. Process shortbread cookies and almonds in a food processor 30 seconds or until finely ground. Place in a medium bowl; stir in melted butter. Press mixture onto bottom of a 9-inch springform pan coated with cooking spray.

2. Bake at 350° for 12 minutes. Cool in pan on a wire rack. Reduce oven temperature to 325°.

3. Prepare Filling: Beat cream cheese and sugar at medium speed with an electric mixer until blended. Add dulce de leche, beating at low speed until blended. Add eggs, 1 at a time, beating just until yellow disappears after each addition. Add pumpkin and next 3 ingredients, beating at low speed until just blended. Pour batter into prepared crust.

4. Bake at 325° for 1 hour and 15 minutes or until almost set. Turn off oven. Let cheesecake stand in oven, with door partially open, 30 minutes. Remove cheesecake from oven, and gently run a knife around edge of cheesecake to loosen from sides of pan. (Do not remove sides of pan.) Cool on a wire rack 1 hour. Cover and chill at least 8 hours.

5. Meanwhile, prepare Candied Almonds: Preheat oven to 300°. Whisk egg white, sugar, and cinnamon until foamy. Fold in almonds until coated. Spread almonds in a single layer on a parchment paper–lined baking sheet.

6. Bake at 300° for 26 to 28 minutes or until golden brown. Cool completely on pan (about 30 minutes). Remove almonds from parchment paper, and break into small pieces.

7. Prepare Topping: Beat ½ cup whipping cream until foamy; gradually add powdered sugar, beating until soft peaks form. Transfer chilled cheesecake to a serving plate. Spread topping over cheesecake.

8. Combine ½ cup dulce de leche and remaining ¼ cup whipping cream in a small saucepan. Cook over low heat, stirring constantly, 4 minutes or until smooth. Drizzle dulce de leche sauce over topping, and sprinkle with Candied Almonds. Serve immediately.

Holiday AFTERNOON TEA

CELEBRATE THE SEASON WITH A FESTIVE
TEA PARTY ENJOYED BY GIRLS
OF ALL AGES.

MENU

Hot Apple Tea

Fig and Bacon Palmiers

Pumpernickel Tea Sandwiches

Smoked Trout and Watercress Tea
Sandwiches

Chicken Salad Tomato Cups

Hazelnut Chip Shortbread

Browned Butter Scones with Faux
Clotted Cream

Buckeye Brownie Cups

Petits Fours Presents

Serves 8

GAME PLAN

1 day before:

- Prepare clotted cream for scones; cover and chill.
- Assemble palmiers; cover and chill, unbaked.
- Prepare filling for pumpernickel sandwiches; cover and chill.
- Toast and skin hazelnuts; store in an airtight container.
- Prepare Buckeye Brownie Cups; store in an airtight container.
- Prepare cake for Petits Fours Presents; wrap airtightly, and chill.

Morning of:

- Prepare shortbread, and bake. Cool; store in an airtight container.
- Prepare cake layers for petits fours; spread with jam. Cover and freeze.
- Prepare chicken salad; cover and chill.
- Prepare filling for smoked trout sandwiches; cover and chill.

2 hours before:

- Prepare scones, and bake.
- Glaze petits fours.

1 hour before:

- Assemble tea sandwiches on a serving tray; cover airtightly, and chill.
- Decorate petits fours.
- Prepare Hot Apple Tea; keep warm.

30 minutes before:

- Slice and bake palmiers; keep warm.
- Assemble Chicken Salad Tomato Cups.
- Set out sandwiches and desserts.

Hot Apple Tea

Makes: 8 servings • Hands-On Time: 5 min. • Total Time: 10 min.

Sweeten with honey or sugar, if desired.

- 3 Tbsp. fresh lemon juice
- ¼ tsp. whole cloves
- ¼ tsp. whole allspice
- 2 (3-inch) cinnamon sticks
- 1 (12-oz.) can frozen apple juice concentrate
- 10 English Breakfast tea bags
- Garnish: thin Granny Smith apple slices

1. Place first 5 ingredients and 8 cups water in a Dutch oven. Bring to a boil, stirring until juice melts; remove from heat. Add tea bags. Cover; steep 5 minutes. Remove tea bags.
2. Pour tea through a strainer, discarding solids. Garnish, if desired.

Fig and Bacon Palmiers

Makes: 32 servings • Hands-On Time: 40 min. • Total Time: 9 hr.

These are the ideal make-ahead recipe for afternoon tea.

- 1 cup chopped small Mission figs
- 1 cup slivered almonds, toasted
- 1 cup (4 oz.) crumbled blue cheese
- 6 oz. cream cheese, softened
- 1 (17.3-oz.) package frozen puff pastry sheets, thawed
- ¼ cup sugar, divided
- 8 bacon slices, cooked, crumbled, and divided
- Parchment paper
- ½ cup fig preserves, finely chopped

1. Process first 2 ingredients in a food processor until finely chopped. Add cheeses; pulse until blended.
2. Carefully unfold 1 sheet of puff pastry on a work surface sprinkled with 2 Tbsp. sugar, pressing out seams.
3. Spread half of cream cheese mixture over pastry to within ½ inch of edges. Press half of bacon into cream cheese mixture. Roll 2 opposite sides, jellyroll fashion, to meet in center. Brush water between rolled sides, and press lightly to seal. Wrap roll in plastic wrap. Repeat procedure with remaining dough, sugar, cream cheese mixture, and bacon. Chill rolls overnight.
4. Preheat oven to 400°.
5. Unwrap rolls. Cut each roll into 16 (½-inch-thick) slices. Place slices 2 inches apart on 2 large baking sheets lined with parchment paper.
6. Bake at 400° for 20 minutes or until golden brown. Immediately brush tops of palmiers with fig preserves. Serve warm.

Hot Apple Tea

Fig and Bacon Palmiers

Pumpernickel Tea Sandwiches

Smoked Trout and Watercress Tea Sandwiches

Pumpernickel Tea Sandwiches

Makes: 21 appetizer servings • Hands-On Time: 15 min. • Total Time: 15 min.

Smear a bit of herb-flavored egg salad on these dainty sandwiches and top them with arugula and radishes.

- 6 large hard-cooked eggs, peeled
- ⅓ cup mayonnaise
- ¼ cup minced fresh chives
- ¼ cup finely chopped fresh mint
- 2 tsp. lemon zest
- 2 tsp. Dijon mustard
- Salt and pepper to taste
- 1⅓ cups loosely packed arugula
- 1 cup very thinly sliced radishes
- 1 Tbsp. lemon juice
- 1 Tbsp. olive oil
- 14 pumpernickel bread slices

1. Mash eggs with mayonnaise and next 4 ingredients until well blended. Season with salt and pepper to taste. Cover and chill up to 1 day.
2. Toss together arugula, radishes, lemon juice, and olive oil. Season with salt and pepper to taste. Toss to coat.
3. Spread egg salad mixture on 1 side of each bread slice; top 7 slices with arugula mixture. Top with remaining 7 bread slices, egg salad side down. Trim crusts from sandwiches; cut each sandwich into 3 rectangles with a serrated knife.

Smoked Trout and Watercress Tea Sandwiches

Makes: 24 appetizer servings • Hands-On Time: 25 min. • Total Time: 25 min.

These delicate finger sandwiches are filled with a creamy smoked trout spread accented with lemon zest, capers, and dill. The spicy watercress offsets the salty, smoky trout while the very thin white bread slices keep the focal point on the star attraction.

- ¼ cup sour cream
- ¼ cup mayonnaise
- 1 Tbsp. finely chopped fresh chives
- 1 tsp. chopped fresh dill
- 1 tsp. chopped drained capers
- ½ tsp. lemon zest
- ¼ tsp. ground white pepper
- 5 oz. smoked trout, skin removed and flaked (1 cup)
- 12 (½-oz.) thin white bread slices, crusts removed
- 1½ cups torn watercress leaves

1. Stir together first 7 ingredients in a medium bowl. Gently fold in trout.
2. Spread ¼ cup trout mixture onto 1 side of each of 6 bread slices. Top each with ¼ cup watercress. Top with remaining bread slices. Cut sandwiches diagonally into quarters.

Chicken Salad
Tomato Cups

Chicken Salad Tomato Cups

Makes: 9 servings • Hands-On Time: 32 min. • Total Time: 37 min.

Shredded chicken salad, paired here with fresh herbs, is served up in delicate tomato cups: perfect finger food for an afternoon tea.

½ cup mayonnaise
⅓ cup finely chopped red onion
⅓ cup finely chopped celery
2 Tbsp. chopped fresh basil
1 Tbsp. chopped fresh chives
1 Tbsp. fresh lemon juice
⅛ tsp. freshly ground pepper
6 oz. deli-roasted chicken, shredded (1½ cups)
18 Campari tomatoes, halved crosswise
Garnish: fresh chives

1. Stir together first 7 ingredients in a medium bowl; gently stir in chicken.
2. Carefully scoop out and discard tomato pulp, leaving a ⅛-inch shell. Place tomato shells upside down on several layers of paper towels; let drain 5 minutes.
3. Spoon about 1 Tbsp. chicken salad into each tomato shell. Garnish, if desired.

Hazelnut Chip Shortbread

Makes: 26 cookies • Hands-On Time: 15 min. • Total Time: 1 hr., 10 min.

Pulsing mini-morsels in a food processor produces little bits of chocolate that freckle the dough.

½ cup semisweet chocolate mini-morsels
1½ cups all-purpose flour
½ cup powdered sugar
½ cup cornstarch
1 cup butter, cut into pieces and softened
½ cup hazelnuts, toasted, chopped, and divided
Parchment paper

1. Preheat oven to 325°. Pulse mini-morsels in a food processor 10 times or until morsels are almost ground. Remove to a bowl. Add flour, powdered sugar, cornstarch, and butter to food processor. Cover; process just until a dough forms and mixture holds its shape. Stir in ¼ cup hazelnuts and ground mini-morsels. Turn dough out onto a lightly floured surface. Roll dough to about ½-inch thickness; cut with a 2-inch scallop-shaped cutter. Press remaining ¼ cup hazelnuts into top of each cookie. Place 1 inch apart on parchment paper-lined baking sheets.
2. Bake at 325° for 18 to 20 minutes or until golden brown. Cool on baking sheets 5 minutes; transfer to wire racks, and cool completely (about 30 minutes).

Note: To toast and skin hazelnuts, place nuts in a single layer in a shallow pan. Bake at 350° for 5 to 10 minutes or until skins begin to split. Transfer warm nuts to a colander; using a towel, rub briskly to remove skins.

Browned Butter Scones with Faux Clotted Cream

Makes: 28 scones • Hands-On Time: 30 min. • Total Time: 2 hr., 20 min.

Browned butter adds depth of flavor to these pure vanilla scones.

- ¾ cup unsalted butter
- 3 cups all-purpose flour
- ⅔ cup sugar
- 1 Tbsp. baking powder
- ½ tsp. salt
- 1 cup whipping cream
- 1 tsp. vanilla extract
- ½ tsp. almond extract
- 1 large egg
- Parchment paper
- 2 Tbsp. whipping cream
- 1 Tbsp. sugar
- Faux Clotted Cream
- Preserves

1. Cook butter in a small heavy saucepan over medium heat, stirring constantly, 6 to 8 minutes or until butter begins to turn golden brown. Remove from heat immediately. Pour butter into a small bowl. Cover and freeze until firm (about 1½ hours).

2. Preheat oven to 425°. Stir together flour, ⅔ cup sugar, baking powder, and salt. Cut in frozen browned butter with a pastry blender until mixture is crumbly. Combine 1 cup whipping cream, extracts, and egg, whisking until blended. Add to flour mixture, stirring with a fork until a shaggy dough forms.

3. Scoop dough by 2 heaping Tbsp. onto parchment paper-lined baking sheets. Brush with 2 Tbsp. whipping cream. Sprinkle with 1 Tbsp. sugar.

4. Bake at 425° for 12 to 14 minutes or until browned. Cool on wire racks. Serve with Faux Clotted Cream and preserves.

Faux Clotted Cream

Makes: 2¼ cups • Hands-On Time: 5 min. • Total Time: 5 min.

This simple version of Devonshire (clotted) cream echoes the taste of the English specialty, but it's quick and easy.

- ½ (8-oz.) container mascarpone cheese, softened
- ¾ cup heavy whipping cream
- 1½ Tbsp. honey
- ½ tsp. vanilla extract

1. Combine all ingredients in a large mixing bowl. Beat at medium speed with an electric mixer until soft peaks form. Store in refrigerator.

Buckeye Brownie Cups

Makes: 32 pieces • Hands-On Time: 37 min. • Total Time: 2 hr., 17 min.

Everything you love in the popular candy bar cups comes together in a decadent cookie. Keep leftover ganache in the refrigerator and use as a topping for ice cream or cake.

32 miniature paper baking cups
1 cup semisweet chocolate morsels, divided
½ cup butter
1½ tsp. vanilla extract, divided
¼ cup firmly packed brown sugar
¼ cup granulated sugar
2 large eggs, lightly beaten
½ cup all-purpose flour
¼ tsp. baking powder
½ cup powdered sugar
½ cup creamy peanut butter
2 Tbsp. butter, softened
¼ cup heavy cream

1. Preheat oven to 350°. Place paper baking cups in miniature muffin pans. Microwave ½ cup chocolate morsels and ½ cup butter in a microwave-safe bowl at HIGH 1 to 2 minutes or until butter melts, stirring after 1 minute. Stir until chocolate melts. Whisk in ½ tsp. vanilla and next 3 ingredients.
2. Combine flour and baking powder; gradually stir into chocolate mixture. Using a small scoop, place 1 level Tbsp. batter in each baking cup. Bake at 350° for 15 minutes. Let cool in pans 5 minutes. Remove from pans to wire racks, and cool completely (about 20 minutes).
3. Meanwhile, combine powdered sugar, peanut butter, 2 Tbsp. softened butter, and remaining 1 tsp. vanilla in a medium bowl; beat at medium speed with an electric mixer until smooth.
4. Roll peanut butter mixture by teaspoonfuls into 32 balls. Press 1 ball into top of each brownie, flattening slightly.
5. Place remaining ½ cup chocolate morsels in a medium bowl. Microwave cream in a 1-cup glass measuring cup at HIGH 1 minute. Pour cream over chocolate morsels; stir until smooth. Let cool until slightly thickened. Spread 1 to 2 tsp. chocolate mixture over peanut butter and brownie, spreading almost to edges of baking cup. Let cool 1 hour or until set.

Petits Fours Presents

Makes: 40 servings • Hands-On Time: 1 hr., 15 min. • Total Time: 5 hr., 30 min.

These tiny morsels made with a dense almond cake and filled with strawberry jam are sure to impress your guests in both taste and presentation. Quick Almond Buttercream can be easily doubled or tripled for decorating layer cakes, cookies, and other baked goods. If you don't want to take the time to make the frosting, simply purchase ready-made frosting at the supermarket.

CAKE
1¼ cups butter, softened
2 cups sugar
1 (7-oz.) tube almond paste
6 large eggs
3 cups all-purpose flour
½ tsp. baking powder
½ tsp. salt
½ cup sour cream
1 tsp. vanilla extract
1 cup strawberry jam

GLAZE
10 cups powdered sugar
¼ cup meringue powder*
1 cup plus 2 Tbsp. half-and-half
2 tsp. almond extract

QUICK ALMOND BUTTERCREAM
½ cup butter, softened
2 cups powdered sugar
2 Tbsp. half-and-half
½ tsp. almond extract
Green food coloring paste

1. Prepare Cake: Preheat oven to 325°. Beat butter at medium speed with an electric mixer until creamy. Gradually add sugar and almond paste; beat 5 minutes or until light and fluffy. Add eggs, 1 at a time, beating until blended after each addition.
2. Combine flour, baking powder, and salt; gradually add to butter mixture alternately with sour cream, beginning and ending with flour mixture. Beat at low speed just until blended after each addition, stopping to scrape bowl as needed. Stir in vanilla. Pour batter into a greased and floured 13- x 9-inch pan.
3. Bake at 325° for 55 minutes or until a wooden pick inserted in center comes out clean. Cool in pan on a wire rack 20 minutes; remove from pan to wire rack, and cool completely (about 1 hour).
4. Trim crusts from all surfaces, making sure top of cake is flat. Slice cake in half horizontally. Spread cut side of bottom half with strawberry jam; replace top half. Cover; freeze 1 hour or until firm.

Buckeye
Brownie Cups

Petits
Fours
Presents

Hazelnut Chip
Shortbread

5. Cut cake into 40 (1½-inch) squares; brush away loose crumbs. Place squares 2 inches apart on wire racks in jelly-roll pans.

6. Prepare Glaze: Beat 10 cups powdered sugar, meringue powder, half-and-half, and almond extract at medium speed with an electric mixer until smooth.

7. Pour glaze over cake squares, completely covering top and sides. Spoon up all excess glaze; continue pouring glaze until all cakes have been covered. Let stand 1 hour or until glaze dries completely.

8. Prepare Quick Almond Buttercream: Beat butter at medium speed with an electric mixer until creamy; gradually add 2 cups powdered sugar, beating until light and fluffy. Add half-and-half

and almond extract; beat 1 minute. Stir in food coloring paste.

9. Trim any excess glaze from bottom of each cake square. Spoon Quick Almond Buttercream into a piping bag fitted with a small round tip, and decorate as desired.

*Note: We tested with Wilton Meringue Powder, which can be found at craft and cake-decorating stores

FIX IT FASTER: Use canned frosting in place of the glaze. Microwave the frosting at HIGH 30 seconds or until pourable. Tint glaze with desired food coloring paste, and follow glaze directions in method.

Brunswick Stew
Benne Seed Cheese Wafers

WINTER IS THE PERFECT TIME OF YEAR
TO ENJOY THIS COZY MEAL HAILING
FROM THE COASTS OF GEORGIA AND
SOUTH CAROLINA.

MENU

Shrimp Pilau

Braised Mustard Greens with
Sausage

Benne Seed Cheese Wafers

Brunswick Stew

Pear-Walnut Huguenot Torte

Serves 6 to 8

1 day before:
- Prepare Benne Seed Cheese Wafers; store in an airtight container.
- Prepare Brandied Cream; cover and chill.
- Peel shrimp; cover and chill.
- Wash, trim, and chop mustard greens; cover and chill.

2 hours before:
- Prepare Brunswick Stew; keep warm.
- Prepare braised greens; keep warm.

1 hour before:
- Prepare Shrimp Pilau; keep warm.
- Prepare Pear-Walnut Huguenot Torte.

Shrimp Pilau

Makes: 6 to 8 servings • Hands-On Time: 20 min. • Total Time: 1 hr., 8 min.

Bacon along with shrimp and tomatoes revs up this classic Lowcountry rice-based dish. Don't be tempted to peek at the rice while it cooks to ensure it's perfectly done.

- 6   bacon slices
- 2   cups chopped sweet onion
- 1   cup chopped celery
- 4   garlic cloves, minced
- ½   tsp. dried crushed red pepper
- 1   (28-oz.) can whole tomatoes, undrained and chopped
- 4   cups chicken broth
- ¼   cup chopped fresh parsley
- 2   Tbsp. chopped fresh oregano
- 1   Tbsp. chopped fresh thyme
- ½   tsp. salt
- ½   tsp. freshly ground pepper
- 2   cups uncooked basmati rice
- 1½   lb. peeled, large raw shrimp (21/25 count)
  Hot sauce

1. Cook bacon in a Dutch oven over medium-high heat 6 to 8 minutes or until crisp; remove bacon from Dutch oven, and drain on paper towels, reserving drippings in Dutch oven. Crumble bacon.

2. Add onion, celery, garlic, and crushed red pepper to drippings in Dutch oven. Cook, stirring often, 5 minutes over medium heat or until vegetables are tender. Add bacon, tomatoes, and next 6 ingredients. Bring to a simmer; add rice. Cover, reduce heat to low, and cook 30 minutes or until liquid is absorbed.

3. Gently stir shrimp into rice; cover and cook 5 more minutes or just until shrimp turn pink. Serve with hot sauce.

Braised Mustard Greens with Sausage

Makes: 6 to 8 servings • Hands-On Time: 15 min. • Total Time: 42 min.

Aromatic garlic and shallots enhance the flavor of cool-weather, peppery mustard greens braised with pork sausage. Crushed red pepper adds heat but can be adjusted to personal taste.

- ½   lb. ground mild Italian sausage
- 1   Tbsp. olive oil
- 2   large shallots, chopped (about ⅓ cup)
- 1   garlic clove, minced
- ½   tsp. dried crushed red pepper
- 1   cup chicken broth
- 2   Tbsp. cider vinegar
- 2   Tbsp. sugar
- 5   large bunches fresh mustard greens (8 to 10 oz. each), washed, trimmed, and chopped (22 cups)
  Salt and pepper to taste

1. Brown sausage in a large Dutch oven over medium-high heat, stirring often, 6 minutes or until meat crumbles and is no longer pink; drain sausage, reserving drippings in pan. Set sausage aside. Add oil to drippings in pan. Add shallots; sauté in hot oil 4 minutes or until tender. Add garlic and crushed red pepper; sauté 1 minute.

2. Stir in chicken broth and next 2 ingredients; bring to a boil. Add half of mustard greens to pan, and cook, stirring constantly, until greens begin to wilt. Add remaining greens, and cook 3 minutes or until greens wilt. Stir in sausage.

3. Reduce heat; cover and simmer 15 minutes or until mustard greens are tender, stirring occasionally. Stir in salt and pepper to taste.

FIX IT FASTER: Use bagged, trimmed, and chopped greens for a shortcut, if desired.

Benne Seed Cheese Wafers

Makes: about 4 dozen • Hands-On Time: 15 min. • Total Time: 27 min.

Sesame seeds are called benne seeds in the southeastern coastal plain region of Georgia and South Carolina's Lowcountry. You can purchase toasted sesame seeds, but for the most flavor, toast your own at 350° for 5 minutes, stirring occasionally. Also, don't be tempted to use preshredded cheese. Shredding it by hand provides softer cheese that holds the dough together.

    1   cup all-purpose flour
    ⅓   cup jarred toasted sesame seeds
    ½   tsp. salt
    ¼   tsp. dry mustard
    ¼   tsp. ground red pepper
    ½   cup butter, softened
    1   (8-oz.) block sharp Cheddar cheese, shredded
    ½   cup jarred toasted sesame seeds (optional)

1. Preheat oven to 350°. Stir together first 5 ingredients in a small bowl.
2. Place butter in a large bowl. Beat at medium speed with an electric mixer until creamy. Add cheese, and beat just until blended. Gradually add flour mixture, beating just until dry ingredients are moistened and a dough forms.
3. Roll dough into 1-inch balls. Roll balls in additional sesame seeds, if desired, pressing gently into dough. Place balls 2 inches apart on ungreased baking sheets; flatten to ⅛-inch thickness with bottom of a glass.
4. Bake at 350° for 12 minutes or until edges are lightly browned.

Pecan Cheese Wafers: Omit sesame seeds. Press a pecan half into each flattened dough ball before baking.

GIFTS FROM THE KITCHEN

Create a special homemade cracker sampler as a gift with recipes throughout the book. Combine Benne Seed Cheese Wafers, Rosemary-Red Wine Wafers (pg. 119), and Wishing Star Cheese Crackers (pg. 120) in a decorative box. Wrap with a ribbon and fasten with a Salt Dough Ornament (pg. 149). This thoughtful gift is sure to spread some holiday cheer!

Brunswick Stew

Makes: 10 cups • Hands-On Time: 18 min. • Total Time: 1 hr., 18 min.

There is an ongoing debate about the origin of this recipe. Some say it was developed in Brunswick County, Virginia. Others swear it was Brunswick, Georgia.

    2   cups frozen cut okra, thawed
    1¾ cups frozen whole kernel corn
    1½ cups frozen baby lima beans
    1½ cups chicken broth
    1   cup smoky barbecue sauce
    1   Tbsp. Worcestershire sauce
    1   tsp. freshly ground pepper
    ½   tsp. salt
    1½ tsp. hot sauce
    1   lb. chopped smoked pulled pork
    1   (28-oz.) can diced tomatoes
    ½   medium onion, chopped

1. Stir together all ingredients in a 6-quart Dutch oven. Cover and bring to a boil; reduce heat, and simmer 1 hour, stirring occasionally.

Pear-Walnut Huguenot Torte

Makes: 8 servings • Hands-On Time: 15 min. • Total Time: 1 hr.

The original Huguenot Torte, hailing from South Carolina, is chock-full of apples and pecans. This version highlights another classic combination—pears and walnuts, and is accented with a hint of spice. It will rise high in the oven while baking and sink as it cools, creating a sweet, sticky pecan pie–like dessert with a meringue crust.

    ¼   cup all-purpose flour
    2½ tsp. baking powder
    ¼   tsp. ground cinnamon
    ⅛   tsp. freshly grated nutmeg
    2   large eggs
    1½ cups sugar
    1   tsp. vanilla extract
    2   cups chopped peeled firm Bartlett pears (about
        3 pears)
    1   cup chopped walnuts, toasted
    Brandied Cream
    Garnish: freshly grated nutmeg

1. Preheat oven to 325°. Generously grease a 13- x 9-inch baking dish.
2. Whisk together first 4 ingredients. Beat eggs at medium

Pear-Walnut
Huguenot Torte

speed with an electric mixer until thick and pale. Gradually add sugar, beating until very light and tripled in volume. Add vanilla; beat until blended. Gradually add flour mixture, beating on low speed just until blended. Fold in pears and walnuts. Pour batter into prepared dish.

3. Bake at 325° for 35 minutes or until golden. Cool 10 minutes. Top with Brandied Cream, and garnish, if desired.

Brandied Cream

Makes: 2 cups • Hands-On Time: 5 min. • Total Time: 5 min.

1 cup whipping cream
3 Tbsp. brandy
2 Tbsp. powdered sugar

1. Beat whipping cream with an electric mixer until foamy; add brandy and powdered sugar, beating until soft peaks form.

Decorate

Get inspired to deck the halls and trim the tree with
these festive ideas to make your home merry.

{1}

Christmas CURB APPEAL

GIVE YOUR GUESTS A MERRY WELCOME AND
BRING HOLIDAY CHEER TO YOUR NEIGHBORHOOD
WITH STELLAR OUTDOOR DECOR.

{2}

{3}

{1} Bring together two holiday decor staples to trim an entrance with classic
white lights and a simple garland made from Fraser fir, Leyland cypress, and cedar.
Adorn boughs of greenery with red and gold ribbon, and tuck branches of ilex
holly berries into everyday planters. {2} Add a little pizzazz to your doorway with
oversized red and white glass balls, strands of sparkly silver beads, and a Douglas
fir garland to create an inviting entrance. {3} Go for the gold with a garland
bedecked with beautiful gold balls, white snowberry branches, and neutral birds.
Add a matching gold satin bow to a Fraser fir wreath for a polished welcome.

{1} Adorn your mailbox with an arrangement of holly, magnolia leaves and fir for a simple spruce-up. {2} Light up a standard lamppost with festive Christmas cheer using fresh or faux Granny Smith apples fastened to a boxwood wreath. {3} Greet your guests with glamorous gates enhanced by bows of green and gold ribbon attached to swags of Christmas tree trimmings. {4} Top a stately brick mailbox with an assortment of fresh fruits, nuts, and clippings from the yard for easy outdoor decor that will last throughout the holiday season. {5} Spread an abundance of glad tidings using the natural charm of fresh greenery and crisp apples to enhance your front door. Extend the apple theme by creating wreaths to spell out "Noel", and display in your yard for all to see.

{1} Have yourself a colorful Christmas using fun, colored balls to brighten a simple wreath and outdoor planters. Tie it all together with a bright green bow for festive flair. {2} Add Christmas inspiration to an outdoor table with a vibrant poinsettia; a simple wreath accented with pinecones, holly berries, and red ribbon; and red ornaments tucked in pots of fresh rosemary. {3} Spread sunshine on colder days with a citrus-inspired setting. These in-season fruits spruce up outdoor decor and require no maintenance. Top clay pots of Christmas paper whites with kumquats. Embellish a fresh wreath with tangerines or oranges. Let your Meyer lemon tree take center stage as a focal point of the room, and dress up a moss-covered reindeer with festive ribbon and clementines for a bow.

{1} Bring the outdoors in with matching loosely arranged
boxwood wreaths to highlight dramatic adjacent windows.
{2} Spread the joy of the season throughout your home with
decorations proclaiming such. Adorn your windows with
white felt ball wreaths for an instant winter wonderland.

{1}

Wonderful WREATHS

WHEN IT COMES TO HOLIDAY DECOR, YOU CAN NEVER HAVE TOO MANY WREATHS. WHETHER OUTDOORS OR INSIDE, WELL-ADORNED WREATHS ADD INSTANT APPEAL THAT WILL BE ENJOYED ALL SEASON LONG.

{2}

{1}

{2}

{3}

{4}

{1} Take a tip from the great outdoors, and give your wreath natural beauty with a medley of pinecones, nuts, and citrus fruits. Create a custom look by forming your wreath into a unique square shape. {2} A combination of blue and white ribbon accents a boxwood wreath for a look that is simple yet stunning. {3} Magnolia leaves, a Southern specialty with sturdiness and shine, create a dazzling door decoration perfect for fall and winter. {4} Whimsical wreaths set a playful tone for the rest of your home during the Christmas season. Bright ribbons and shimmering accents give festive flair to traditional greenery in this contemporary creation. {5} Silver stars and matching ribbon adorn simple evergreen for an elegant entrance that is twice as nice.

{5}

A Welcoming ENTRANCE

MAKE A FABULOUS FIRST IMPRESSION WITH A FESTIVE FOYER THAT YOUR GUESTS ARE SURE TO REMEMBER.

{1} Set up a miniature winter wonderland to gladly welcome your guests. These timeless treasures can be easily arranged against your ordinary entry table display. {2} This precious pooch perched next to your front door stands ready to provide a cheerful welcome and won't hop on guests! Fix up Fido with a little greenery and a fitting gold bow to harmonize with the rest of your holiday decor. {3} Draping greenery from the top to the bottom of your foyer will infuse your home with the seasonal scent of fresh fir, pine, cypress, and cedar to be enjoyed all season long. A serene nativity scene provides a remembrance of the true meaning of Christmas at your entrance.

{1} Beautify your banister with a collection of natural accents for a woodsy welcome. {2} You won't have to go far to create a dazzling display. Simply gather a collection of pinecones, unique feathers, boxwood greenery, and citrus fruits for a perfectly polished banister. {3} A rustic white mirror and vintage accents are all you need for an easy but elegant entry table. A collection of candles provides an inviting glow, and a potted paperwhite surrounded by Granny Smith apples is sure to offer a warm welcome. {4} Your wreaths don't have to stop at the door. Eucalyptus wreaths descending the staircase give a unique holiday touch with plenty of seasonal splendor from dainty lady apples and handsome striped bows.

{1}

{1} Contemporary angel figurines, an array of elegant candles, and assorted flowers fashion an inviting entrance that is sure to impress. A framed chalkboard heralds events to come.

{2} The shimmer of silver is all it takes to create a stately styled entry table. Pinecones decoratively hung from a large mirror and a simple white and green arrangement of bells of Ireland, hydrangea, and snapdragons pulls the look together for a beautiful hallway display.

Merry MANTELS

TURN YOUR MANTEL INTO A
MEMORABLE, EYE-CATCHING FOCAL
POINT WITH ENOUGH CHARM TO DRAW
FAMILY AND FRIENDS NEAR.

{1}

{1} Nature receives a nod with this festive fireplace. A
pine and cedar garland is enhanced with earthy accents
such as rustic pinecones, strung nuts in their shells, and
ruby red holly berries to give this mantel natural sophisti-
cation. {2} Tones of red, green, and gold create an inviting
atmosphere with a festive feel. The color scheme, taste-
fully repeated in accents throughout the room, is a perfect
match for this foresty fireplace.

{2}

{1} Don't be afraid to shy away from ordinary evergreen in order to transform your mantel into an organic masterpiece. Combining Southern staples such as fluffy white cotton and bold red pomegranates dresses up a mantel with impeccable style. {2} The simple combination of blushing crab apples and flowing Leyland cypress plays up a mantel that already boasts of style and charm. Accent the look with sage green and neutral brown-and-green–striped ribbon to bring the whole concept together.

{1}

{1} Bright colors bring fun to any room, especially at Christmastime. Matching polka dot stockings pair perfectly with colorful Christmas trees to make this mantel even merrier. {2} White roses are a wonderful way to elegantly enhance your mantel. Simply place them in silver mint julep cups atop fresh Douglas fir for a tasteful touch of seasonal aroma. {3} Create a traditional mantel accented by modern elements. Cherished mono-grammed stockings and ceramic holders brightly play against neutral nutcrackers and contemporary artwork for a truly timeless display.

{2}

3

Cheery
CHRISTMAS TREES

A PERFECTLY TRIMMED TREE IS THE ESSENTIAL CENTERPIECE OF YOUR HOLIDAY HOME. WHETHER TRADITIONAL OR TRENDY, YOU CAN CREATE A STYLE THAT'S ALL YOUR OWN.

{1}

{1} Keeping your color scheme consistent creates an alluring atmosphere while allowing your tree to twinkle. Subtle green, brown, and gold bring the outdoors into your living room for a relaxing setting inspired by nature. {2} Bigger is better, brighter, and more beautiful when it comes to this phenomenal fir bedecked with sparkling crystal ornaments. Gorgeous gold-trimmed armchairs dressed with miniature wreaths are an exquisite accompaniment to the tree's beauty.

{2}

{1} A Christmas classic, candy canes are the perfect pairing with your acquired collection of brightly colored holiday ornaments. The red and white in the time-honored treat allows your ornament collection to shine while keeping a festive Christmas color scheme. {2} Going out of the ordinary results in the extraordinary as earthy elements couple with contemporary Christmas ornaments in this woodsy wonder. {3} Brown paper packages tied up in plaid bring together some of our favorite things for completing your Christmas tree. {4} A sheer red ribbon cascading to the floor adds a final flourish to a perfectly trimmed tree that's sure to delight your family and friends.

{4}

{3}

Timeless TABLE SETTINGS

SET A MERRY MOOD BY PERFECTLY DRESSING THE DINING ROOM FOR YOUR HOLIDAY FEAST.

{1} Shimmering snowflakes will warm the hearts of your guests as they sit down to enjoy time together. {2} Timeless silver and gold china lends a traditional touch to your dinner table. The dazzling color scheme is continued with simple arrangements of metallic-sprayed branches. {3} Ravishing red tulips in a grand mercury glass vase and surrounded by sparkling mercury glass Christmas trees add a pop of color that stands out among modern and traditional dining decor.

{1} A neutral palette of white and green or gold and silver sets the mood for a tasteful table setting that is worthy of holiday gatherings all season long. {2} Arrangements of white tulips and ranunculus create a pristine appearance throughout your dining room. Place the white blooms in mercury glass votives and fasten them to the chandelier with floral wire and brown ribbons. {3} Surround an assortment of white hydrangeas, tulips, and ranunculus with a fresh wreath to give your table timeless romantic appeal. {4} A collection of descending candles surrounded by boxwood, lady apples, white tulips, hydrangeas, and dusty miller illuminates your dining room in a way that will dazzle your guests.

{1}

{1} Your holiday brunch will be one to remember with a natural setting that is inviting yet inexpensive to put together. Take a walk outside to collect the holly and rosemary for a setting that allows you to enjoy the outdoors while staying warm inside. Show your unique style with artful antique bowls. {2} Go green in your kitchen with an effortless fresh bay leaf wreath hung over a rustic table. A pair of miniature boxwood trees are the center of attention and help achieve a cozy country style your family will enjoy.

{2}

{4}

{3} Bring together the old and the new using antique accents with contemporary flair. A chalkboard announces the evening meal, and two topiaries flank the table for an eclectic table setting you can leave up all winter long. {4} Treat your guests to a wonderful holiday meal with a whimsical iron rooster at the heart of your table. Monogrammed napkins and plate markers provide a personalized touch.

{1} Celebrate the season with striking dining room decor accentuated by Christmas red and green. An impressive bouquet of red tulips, roses, snapdragons, miniature callas, pepperberries, and orchids serves as a superb centerpiece beneath a lavishly dressed chandelier. {2} Think pink when creating a breathtakingly beautiful table setting that exhibits over-the-top elegance. Pink-tinged goblets and plates are the perfect complement for this grand display. The bright hue of the peonies brings out the charm of traditional china and the magnificent crystal chandelier. {3} Showcase pretty pink peonies by putting the blooms in glass vases of various sizes and placing the arrangements at the center of the table. A hint of fresh mistletoe is the essential accompaniment.

{3}

{2}

{3}

Old to NEW AGAIN

DECORATING FOR CHRISTMAS DOESN'T HAVE TO CUT INTO YOUR HOLIDAY SPENDING. GET CREATIVE USING ELEMENTS FROM CHRISTMASES PAST AND TRY UNUSUAL USES FOR EVERYDAY ITEMS.

{1}

{1} A collection of vintage kitchen gadgets makes an adorable, unexpected wreath for your kitchen window. {2} Combine your everyday kitchen decor with on-hand items for a fun, fuss-free flourish. Mounds of fluffy marshmallows soften your place settings while white letters spell out the spirit of Christmas in your kitchen. Hang glass balls of all sizes from your ceiling to collect the morning light and bring sparkle to the room. {3} Bring an antique bathtub to your kitchen for a surprising window box display. Pretty paperwhites and pansies can be planted to coordinate with the white porcelain. {4} A rustic door and bench placed in your kitchen form the perfect backdrop for a casual look. The country-style bench serves as a handy storage unit for gift baskets or other decor.

{2}

{3}

{4}

{1}

{2}

{1} Bundle antique silverware with twine and fasten to cabinet handles and drawer pulls for a delightfully decorative touch that's out of the ordinary. {2} Create the perfect space for holiday baking. Flea market-found baking gadgets, a green Depression glass cake stand, and a strand of lights inspire a cozy lived-in look. {3} Layer a bit of old and new for an old-fashioned Christmas countertop. You can use what you already have in addition to flea market finds. Antique dishes are an excellent way to bring a vintage Christmas theme to your home. Store dinner rolls and breads in a rustic breadbox alongside vintage flour and sugar canisters for holiday baking. A simple nativity scene adds an extra special touch to remind all of the reason for the season.

{3}

A Child's
CHRISTMAS

DECORATE YOUR CHILD'S ROOM WITH HOLIDAY CHEER TO HEIGHTEN THE EXCITEMENT OF SANTA'S IMPENDING ARRIVAL. BRIGHTEN THE SPACE WITH THEIR FAVORITE COLORS AND SEASONAL WHIMSICAL TOUCHES.

{1} A noble nutcracker guards this boldly decorated boy's room while miniature nutcrackers placed throughout serve as the inspiration for the gold fringe and plaid palette. {2} Make a ballerina tutu tree by arranging pale pink tulle around a foam craft cone. String Christmas lights over a closet door and add brightly colored ribbons tied around the strand. {3} This fun, curly Christmas tree adds an artsy, whimsical touch to a child's room or play area. {4} A pretty pink corner is perfect for any princess. Decorate small pink and green tinsel trees with matching ornaments and white lights for girly flair. Pair with presents wrapped in coordinating shades.

{4}

{1}

{2}

JOY TO THE WORLD!

{3}

{4}

{1} With a little creativity and childlike wonder, you can create a charming play area that will be adored by children and adults. Don't hold back when it comes to transforming kids' spaces into something they will treasure. {2} This fun felt wreath adds a multitude of color to a child's bedroom or play area. {3} Hang brightly colored wall accents in different shapes and sizes for a delightful display. {4} A trio of wooden ornaments hanging from a door or window brightens a comfy corner area. {5} Try displaying a variety of Christmas crafts on shelves in a child's room or play area. The kids can even help construct some of the crafts to be displayed. {6} An out-of-the-ordinary element such as this curved Christmas tree adds a little festive fun to the room. Multicolored lights echo the whimsy.

{5}

{6}

Savor

From easy appetizers and hearty main dishes
to showstopping desserts, this abundant
collection of inspiring recipes can be
enjoyed year-round.

Easy
BAKED
BREAKFAST

LET THE OVEN DO THE WORK DURING
THIS BUSY TIME OF YEAR. YOU'RE SURE
TO START THE DAY OFF RIGHT WITH
THESE SUNNY SENSATIONS.

Loaded Hash Brown Quiche

(pictured on facing page)
Makes: 6 servings • Hands-On Time: 20 min. • Total Time: 1 hr., 45 min.

Shredded hash browns make a unique crust for this classic-flavored quiche.

  4   cups (½ [22-oz.] package) frozen shredded
      hash browns, thawed
  ½   tsp. salt
  ½   tsp. freshly ground pepper
  6   large eggs
1¼   cups heavy cream
  ¾   cup milk
  2   cups (8 oz.) shredded sharp Cheddar cheese
  ½   cup chopped green onions
  8   cooked bacon slices, crumbled
  ½   cup sour cream

1. Preheat oven to 400°. Lightly grease a 9-inch deep-dish pie plate. Stir together hash browns, salt, and pepper in a medium bowl. Press seasoned hash browns on bottom and up sides of pie plate, forming a crust. Bake at 400° for 15 minutes or until lightly browned. Let cool 5 minutes. Reduce oven temperature to 350°.
2. Whisk together eggs, heavy cream, and milk. Pour egg mixture into hash brown crust. Sprinkle with cheese, green onions, and bacon.
3. Bake at 350° for 1 hour and 10 minutes to 1 hour and 20 minutes or until set, shielding edges with aluminum foil after 1 hour to prevent excessive browning. Top each serving with a dollop of sour cream.

DON'T TOSS OUT THAT BREAD!

Strata and baked French toast recipes are great for using day-old crusty bread that may have become stale. The bread is dry enough to soak up the custard yet not get soggy. If you don't have any stale bread, it's easy to make. Simply cube the bread, spread it in one layer on a baking sheet, and let it stand uncovered for 8 to 24 hours.

Butternut Squash Strata with Smoked Bacon

Makes: 8 servings • Hands-On Time: 25 min. • Total Time: 1 hr., 25 min.

Butternut squash has found its way onto the holiday table in soups, sides, and even pies. Why not make it the star of your next brunch?

  8   large eggs, lightly beaten
2½   cups half-and-half
  2   tsp. Dijon mustard
  3   Tbsp. chopped fresh sage
  1   tsp. salt
  ¼   tsp. freshly ground pepper
  8   cups cubed sourdough bread, divided (about
      1 [16-oz.] loaf)
  1   cup (4 oz.) shredded provolone cheese, divided
  ⅔   cup (3 oz.) freshly shredded Parmesan cheese, divided
  8   hickory-smoked bacon slices
  ¼   cup butter, divided
  3   shallots, thinly sliced (¾ cup)
  2   (10-oz.) packages cubed butternut squash, thawed
      (4 cups)

1. Preheat oven to 350°. Whisk together eggs and half-and-half in a large bowl. Stir in mustard, sage, salt, and pepper. Stir in 7 cups bread cubes. Stir in ¾ cup provolone cheese and ⅓ cup Parmesan cheese. Let stand 20 minutes.
2. Meanwhile, cook bacon in a large nonstick skillet over medium heat 8 minutes or until crisp; remove from skillet, and drain on paper towels, reserving 2 Tbsp. drippings in skillet. Coarsely crumble bacon.
3. Melt 2 Tbsp. butter in skillet with hot drippings. Add shallots, and cook over medium heat, stirring often, 2 minutes or until tender. Add squash, and toss gently to coat. Add squash mixture and bacon to bread mixture; pour into a greased 13- x 9-inch baking dish.
4. Pulse remaining 1 cup bread cubes in a food processor 3 or 4 times or until coarsely crumbled. Combine breadcrumbs and remaining 2 Tbsp. butter, ¼ cup provolone cheese, and ⅓ cup Parmesan cheese in skillet, tossing with any remaining bacon drippings; sprinkle over strata.
5. Bake at 350° for 45 minutes or until lightly browned and set. Let stand 5 minutes before serving.

Ham and Cheese
Croissant Strata

QUICK & EASY
Bacon-and-Cheddar Frittata

Makes: 4 servings • Hands-On Time: 22 min. • Total Time: 29 min.

A frittata is an Italian-style flat omelet. Though it can be made with many complex ingredients, this is a simple and easy version.

- ¼ cup milk
- ⅛ tsp. freshly ground pepper
- 8 large eggs
- 8 bacon slices
- 6 oz. (1½ cups) sharp Cheddar cheese, shredded and divided
- 3 green onions, sliced

1. Preheat broiler. Whisk together first 3 ingredients until well blended.
2. Cook bacon, in batches, in a 10-inch cast-iron skillet over medium-high heat 8 minutes or until crisp; remove bacon, reserving 1 Tbsp. drippings. Crumble bacon. Whisk bacon, 1 cup cheese, and green onions into egg mixture. Cook egg mixture in hot drippings, without stirring, 5 minutes or until bottom of mixture begins to set; sprinkle with remaining ½ cup cheese. Broil 6 inches from heat 2 minutes or just until puffy and cheese melts. Serve immediately.

Ham and Cheese Croissant Strata

Makes: 6 servings • Hands-On Time: 15 min. • Total Time: 50 min.

Start a new holiday breakfast tradition this year by serving this cheesy ham bake, reminiscent of the famous French sandwich, Croque Monsieur.

- 6 croissants, split
- 6 (¾- or 1-oz.) Swiss cheese slices
- 2 cups chopped deli ham
- 8 large eggs
- 1½ cups milk
- 2 tsp. Dijon mustard
- ¼ tsp. salt
- ¼ tsp. pepper
- 1 cup (4 oz.) shredded Gruyère cheese
- Garnish: chopped fresh chives

1. Preheat oven to 350°. Arrange bottom halves of croissants, cut sides up, in a single layer in a lightly greased 13- x 9-inch baking dish. Top each croissant with 1 cheese slice. Sprinkle with ham. Top with remaining croissant halves, cut sides down.
2. Whisk together eggs and next 4 ingredients in a large bowl. Pour egg mixture over croissants. Sprinkle with Gruyère cheese.
3. Bake at 350° for 35 minutes or until browned and set. Garnish, if desired. Serve immediately.

Smoked Sausage and Vegetable Strata

Makes: 8 servings • Hands-On Time: 35 min. • Total Time: 1 hr., 50 min., plus 16 hr. for chilling and standing

This make-ahead breakfast strata gets a flavor boost from spicy andouille sausage. Sautéed onions, peppers, and mushrooms, along with a blend of cheeses, round out this hearty dish. Serve it with hot pepper sauce for the guests who like to raise the heat a notch.

 6 oz. French bread, cut into 8 (1-inch-thick) slices
 1 lb. andouille sausage, cut into ½-inch slices*
1½ cups chopped onion
1½ cups coarsely chopped red bell pepper
 1 (8-oz.) package baby portobello mushrooms, sliced
1½ tsp. chopped fresh thyme
 1 cup (4 oz.) shredded sharp Cheddar cheese
 1 cup (4 oz.) shredded fontina cheese
 6 large eggs, lightly beaten
1½ cups milk
 1 tsp. salt
 ¼ tsp. freshly ground pepper
   Garnish: chopped fresh parsley

1. Arrange bread slices in a single layer on a baking sheet. Let stand, uncovered, 8 to 24 hours.

2. Cut sausage slices in half. Cook sausage, in batches, in a large skillet over medium-high heat, stirring often, 4 minutes or until browned. Remove sausage from skillet using a slotted spoon; reserve drippings in skillet. Add onion and red bell pepper to hot drippings; sauté 4 minutes or until tender. Add sliced mushrooms and thyme; sauté 6 minutes or until liquid evaporates.

3. Cut bread into 1-inch cubes (about 7 cups cubed). Arrange bread cubes in a lightly greased 13- x 9-inch baking dish. Top with onion mixture and sausage. Sprinkle with cheeses.

4. Whisk together eggs and next 3 ingredients in a bowl; pour over bread mixture. Cover and chill 8 to 16 hours.

5. Preheat oven to 350°. Let baking dish stand at room temperature 30 minutes. Uncover and bake 45 to 55 minutes or until puffed and golden. Let stand 5 minutes before serving. Garnish, if desired.

*Spicy smoked sausage, cut into ½-inch slices, may be substituted.

Gouda-Pancetta Grits Casserole

Makes: 6 servings • Hands-On Time: 15 min. • Total Time: 1 hr.

This dressed-up grits casserole is a diversion from the everyday Cheddar and bacon variety. Don't save this recipe only for breakfast or brunch—it's also great as a side for pork chops or filets.

    2   oz. pancetta, finely chopped
    1   shallot, minced
    2   cups chicken broth
    1   cup half-and-half
    1   cup uncooked quick-cooking grits
    ½   cup grated Asiago cheese
    8   oz. Gouda cheese, shredded
    ¼   tsp. freshly ground pepper
    ⅛   tsp. hot sauce
    2   large eggs, lightly beaten

1. Preheat oven to 350°. Cook pancetta in a large skillet over medium-high heat 3 minutes or until crisp; remove pancetta, and drain on paper towels, reserving drippings in skillet. Sauté shallot in hot drippings until tender.

2. Bring broth and half-and-half to a boil in a large saucepan; stir in grits. Return to a boil; cover, reduce heat, and simmer 5 minutes, stirring occasionally. Remove from heat; add cheeses, pepper, and hot sauce, stirring until cheeses melt. Stir in pancetta, shallots, and eggs.

3. Spoon grits mixture into a lightly greased 11- x 7-inch baking dish. Bake at 350° for 45 minutes or until set and lightly browned.

Andouille and Spinach Pie

Makes: 8 servings • Hands-On Time: 14 min. • Total Time: 1 hr., 40 min.

Serve this savory dish with fresh fruit and mimosas for a New Orleans-style brunch.

    1   lb. andouille sausage, chopped
    8   large eggs
    ½   cup heavy cream
    2   (8-oz.) packages shredded Italian six-cheese blend or
        1 (16-oz.) package shredded mozzarella-provolone
        cheese blend
    ½   tsp. salt
    2   (6-oz.) packages fresh baby spinach
    2   garlic cloves, minced
    1   (14.1-oz.) package refrigerated piecrusts
    1   egg yolk

Andouille and Spinach Pie

1. Preheat oven to 375°. Cook sausage in a large Dutch oven over medium heat, stirring often, 5 minutes or until browned; remove sausage, reserving drippings in Dutch oven.

2. Meanwhile, whisk eggs and heavy cream in a large bowl. Stir in cheese blend and salt.

3. Add spinach and garlic to reserved drippings, and cook 1½ minutes, stirring constantly, until all spinach has wilted. Add spinach and sausage to cheese mixture, stirring well.

4. Fit 1 piecrust into a 9-inch deep-dish pie plate or 10-inch pie plate according to package directions. Spoon sausage-spinach mixture into piecrust. Fit remaining piecrust over filling mixture; gently press edges, sealing to bottom piecrust. Fold edges under, and crimp.

5. Whisk together egg yolk and 1 Tbsp. water; brush over piecrust. Cut slits in top for steam to escape. Bake at 375° for 1 hour or until golden brown. Let stand 15 minutes before serving.

Pear-Hazelnut French Toast

Makes: 8 servings • Hands-On Time: 25 min. • Total Time: 1 hr., 10 min., plus 16 hours for chilling and standing

Sweet caramel and tender winter pears, reminiscent of a Poire Tarte, make for a decadent French toast. Best of all, this breakfast is prepared the night before, allowing the bread to absorb the vanilla-scented custard and "the cook" to sleep in or enjoy precious family time.

- 1 (16-oz.) French bread loaf, cut into 16 (1½-inch-thick) slices
- 8 Tbsp. butter, divided
- 6 Bartlett pears (about 2½ lb.), peeled and cut into 8 wedges each
- 1 cup firmly packed brown sugar
- 3 Tbsp. light corn syrup
- 6 large eggs, lightly beaten
- 2 cups milk
- 2 Tbsp. hazelnut liqueur
- 1 tsp. vanilla extract
- ⅛ tsp. freshly ground nutmeg
- ⅛ tsp. salt
- ½ cup chopped hazelnuts, toasted
- Powdered sugar
- Maple syrup, warmed

1. Arrange bread slices in a single layer on a baking sheet. Let stand, uncovered, 8 to 24 hours.
2. Melt 2 Tbsp. butter in a large nonstick skillet over medium heat. Add pears, and cook, stirring occasionally, 10 minutes or until pears are crisp-tender and just beginning to brown.

Pear-Hazelnut French Toast

3. Meanwhile, microwave remaining 6 Tbsp. butter in a microwave-safe bowl at HIGH 45 seconds. Stir in brown sugar and corn syrup. Spread mixture in a lightly greased 13- x 9-inch baking dish. Place cooked pears in an even layer over top.
4. Whisk together eggs and next 5 ingredients in a large bowl. Dip both sides of bread slices into egg mixture, coating well. Place bread slices, side by side, in a single layer over pears. Pour remaining egg mixture over top. Cover and chill 8 to 12 hours.
5. Preheat oven to 350°. Let baking dish stand while oven heats. Uncover and bake 45 minutes or until golden brown. Sprinkle with hazelnuts and powdered sugar. Serve immediately with warm maple syrup.

Turkey Club Breakfast Casserole

Makes: 8 to 10 servings • Hands-On Time: 21 min. • Total Time: 51 min.

An excellent way to use up leftover Herb- and Citrus-Glazed Turkey (page 29).

- 2½ cups half-and-half, divided
- 1 (5-oz.) package garlic butter–flavored croutons (3 cups)
- 12 bacon slices, cut crosswise into ¼-inch strips
- 1 cup chopped green bell pepper
- ½ cup chopped onion
- 8 large eggs
- ¼ tsp. salt
- ⅛ tsp. freshly ground pepper
- 2 (8-oz.) packages shredded Italian six-cheese blend, divided
- 2½ cups coarsely chopped cooked turkey
- Garnish: halved grape tomatoes, chopped fresh parsley

1. Preheat oven to 350°. Stir together 1½ cups half-and-half and croutons in a medium bowl until croutons are thoroughly coated. Let stand 8 minutes.
2. Cook bacon in a large skillet over medium-high heat 7 to 8 minutes or until crisp; remove bacon, and drain on paper towels, reserving 2 Tbsp. drippings in skillet. Crumble bacon. Cook green pepper and onion in hot drippings 6 minutes or until tender, stirring often.
3. Whisk together eggs and next 2 ingredients in a large bowl; whisk in remaining 1 cup half-and-half. Spoon crouton mixture into bottom of a lightly greased 13- x 9-inch baking dish; sprinkle with 1 package cheese. Top with turkey, bacon, and bell pepper mixture. Pour egg mixture over turkey mixture.
4. Bake at 350° for 25 minutes or until set and lightly browned. Sprinkle with remaining cheese. Bake 5 more minutes or until cheese melts. Let stand 5 minutes. Garnish, if desired.

Chocolate-Hazelnut Glazed Doughnuts

Makes: 12 servings • Hands-On Time: 20 min. • Total Time: 50 min.

As an option, you can dust these cake doughnuts with powdered sugar or dip them in cinnamon sugar.

1½ cups cake flour
⅔ cup sugar
½ cup white whole wheat flour
2 tsp. baking powder
1 tsp. freshly grated nutmeg
½ tsp. salt
¾ cup buttermilk
¼ cup canola oil
1 Tbsp. vanilla bean paste*
2 large eggs
½ cup sour cream
Vegetable cooking spray
1 cup hazelnut spread
½ cup finely chopped hazelnuts, toasted

1. Preheat oven to 425°. Stir together cake flour and next 5 ingredients until well blended.

2. Combine buttermilk, canola oil, vanilla bean paste, and eggs just until blended. Stir in sour cream. Gradually add buttermilk mixture to flour mixture, stirring just until blended. Let batter stand 10 minutes. Coat 2 (6-cup) nonstick doughnut pans with cooking spray. Spoon batter into prepared pans.

3. Bake at 425° for 9 to 10 minutes or until doughnuts spring back when lightly touched. Cool in pans 3 minutes; remove from pans to wire racks. Spread each doughnut with 1 rounded Tbsp. hazelnut spread; dip in hazelnuts.

*Vanilla extract may be substituted.

Note: We tested with Nutella hazelnut spread. If you have only one doughnut pan, then bake the doughnuts in batches, chilling the batter between each batch.

Blintz Casserole with Blueberry Sauce

Makes: 12 servings • Hands-On Time: 20 min. • Total Time: 1 hr., 20 min., including sauce

Making individual blintzes can be time consuming and intimidating. Enjoy the flavor of a rolled blintz in a casserole that's quick and easy to make.

FILLING
- 1 (8-oz.) package cream cheese, softened
- ⅓ cup granulated sugar
- 1 large egg
- 1 (15-oz.) container ricotta cheese
- 2 tsp. lemon zest
- 1½ Tbsp. lemon juice
- ⅛ tsp. salt

TOPPING
- ¼ cup granulated sugar
- ¼ cup firmly packed brown sugar
- ½ tsp. ground cinnamon

BATTER
- ¾ cup all-purpose flour
- ⅓ cup granulated sugar
- 2 tsp. baking powder
- ⅛ tsp. salt
- 2 large eggs, lightly beaten
- ½ cup butter, melted
- 3 Tbsp. milk
- 1 tsp. vanilla extract

REMAINING INGREDIENTS
Sweetened whipped cream
Blueberry Sauce
Garnish: fresh mint

1. Preheat oven to 325°. Prepare Filling: Beat cream cheese and ⅓ cup sugar at medium speed with an electric mixer until smooth. Add egg, and beat on low speed just until blended. Add ricotta and next 3 ingredients, beating at medium speed just until blended.

2. Prepare Topping: Stir together granulated sugar and next 2 ingredients in a small bowl.

3. Prepare Batter: Whisk together flour and next 3 ingredients in a bowl. Whisk together eggs and next 3 ingredients; gradually add egg mixture to flour mixture, whisking until blended.

4. Pour ¾ cup batter into a greased 13- x 9-inch baking dish. Spoon filling over batter. Dollop remaining batter (about 1 cup) over filling; spread batter to edges of baking dish. Sprinkle topping over batter.

5. Bake at 325° for 40 to 45 minutes or until lightly browned and set. Let cool 10 minutes. Serve warm with whipped cream and Blueberry Sauce. Garnish, if desired.

Blueberry Sauce

Makes: 2¾ cups • Hands-On Time: 10 min. • Total Time: 10 min.

- 1 (10-oz.) package frozen blueberries, thawed (2¾ cups)
- ¼ cup sugar
- 2 Tbsp. lemon juice
- 1 tsp. lemon zest
- 1 Tbsp. cornstarch

1. Combine first 4 ingredients in a medium saucepan. Bring to a boil over medium heat, stirring often.

2. Combine cornstarch and 1 Tbsp. water; add to blueberry mixture. Cook, stirring constantly, until slightly thickened.

Tip: Blueberry Sauce can be made the day ahead and reheated.

Festive
PIES & TARTS

PROVIDE THE PERFECT ENDING TO
ANY HOLIDAY MEAL WITH THESE
YULETIDE DESSERTS.

Clementine Custard Shortbread Tart

(pictured on facing page)
Makes: 12 servings • Hands-On Time: 30 min. • Total Time: 2 hr., including custard and syrup

Blood oranges would be equally delicious in this elegant tart.

- ¾ cup butter, softened
- ⅓ cup granulated sugar
- ⅛ tsp. almond extract
- 1½ cups all-purpose flour
- ½ cup finely ground almonds
- ⅛ tsp. salt
- Vanilla Custard
- 18 peeled clementines, cut into ¼-inch slices (2¼ lb.)
- Clementine Syrup
- Garnish: pomegranate seeds

1. Beat butter at medium speed with an electric mixer until creamy. Add sugar and almond extract, beating until blended. Stir together flour, almonds, and salt; gradually add to butter mixture, beating at low speed just until blended. Flatten dough into a disk. Wrap in plastic wrap, and chill 30 minutes.
2. Press dough evenly into bottom and up sides of a 10-inch tart pan with removable bottom; trim excess pastry. Freeze 10 minutes.
3. Preheat oven to 350°. Line pastry with aluminum foil, and fill with pie weights or dried beans.
4. Bake at 350° for 30 minutes. Remove weights and foil. Cool on a wire rack.
5. Spoon Vanilla Custard into cooled crust. Arrange clementine slices, slightly overlapping, on top of tart to cover filling completely. Brush fruit with Clementine Syrup. Serve immediately. Cover and store leftovers in refrigerator. Garnish, if desired.

Vanilla Custard

Makes: 2½ cups • Hands-On Time: 10 min. • Total Time: 25 min.

- ½ cup sugar
- 3 Tbsp. cornstarch
- 2 cups whipping cream
- 6 egg yolks
- 1 vanilla bean

1. Whisk together sugar and cornstarch in a heavy saucepan. Whisk in cream and egg yolks. Split vanilla bean lengthwise, and scrape out seeds. Stir seeds into cream mixture, reserving bean for Clementine Syrup. Bring to a boil over medium heat, whisking constantly. Boil, whisking constantly, 1 minute or until thickened. Remove pan from heat.
2. Place pan in ice water; whisk occasionally until cool.

Clementine Syrup

Makes: about ¼ cup • Hands-On Time: 7 min. • Total Time: 22 min.

- Reserved vanilla bean from Vanilla Custard
- ¼ cup sugar
- 1 clementine, cut into ¼-inch slices
- 1 Tbsp. orange liqueur

1. Combine vanilla bean, sugar, and 2 Tbsp. water in a small saucepan. Squeeze juice from clementine slices into sugar mixture. Add squeezed clementine slices to mixture. Bring to a boil. Reduce heat to medium-low; simmer, stirring occasionally, 10 minutes or until syrup thickens. Remove from heat, and let cool. Pour clementine mixture through a fine wire-mesh strainer into a bowl; discard solids. Stir in liqueur.

Rum Raisin-Coconut Pies

Makes: 16 servings • Hands-On Time: 20 min. • Total Time: 3 hr., 40 min.

This recipe makes two pies, one to enjoy and one to give away.

- 2 cups raisins
- ½ cup dark rum
- 1 (14.1-oz.) package refrigerated piecrusts
- ½ cup unsalted butter, melted and cooled
- 1½ cups sugar
- 4 large eggs
- 1 (14-oz.) can coconut milk
- 2 cups sweetened shredded coconut
- ½ cup self-rising flour
- 2 oz. dark chocolate (optional)

1. Preheat oven to 425°. Soak raisins in rum.
2. Meanwhile, roll 1 piecrust into a 13-inch circle on a flat surface. Fit into a 9-inch pie plate; fold edges under, and crimp. Repeat procedure with remaining piecrust, fitting into a second 9-inch pie plate.
3. Bake piecrusts at 425° for 10 minutes. Transfer to a wire rack, and cool 20 minutes. Reduce oven temperature to 350°.
4. Whisk together butter, sugar, and eggs in a large bowl until mixture is well blended. Add coconut milk and next 2 ingredients; stir until well blended. Drain raisins, and fold into butter mixture. Pour into prepared crusts.
5. Bake at 350° for 47 to 50 minutes or until a knife inserted in center comes out clean. Transfer pies to wire racks, and cool completely (about 2 hours).
6. Melt dark chocolate in a microwave-safe bowl at MEDIUM (50% power) 1 minute or until melted and smooth, stirring at 30-second intervals. Drizzle over pies, if desired.

MAKE AHEAD
Butterscotch-Pecan Tassies

Makes: 24 servings • Hands-On Time: 11 min. • Total Time: 2 hr., 16 min. (including pastry)

Here's an old-fashioned dessert with a butterscotch flavor twist that's sure to be a hit with all ages.

½ cup butterscotch morsels
2 Tbsp. butter
⅓ cup light corn syrup
2 large eggs
⅓ cup firmly packed light brown sugar
2 tsp. vanilla extract
½ cup chopped pecans
Cream Cheese Pastry

1. Preheat oven to 350°. Microwave butterscotch morsels and butter in a microwave-safe bowl at MEDIUM HIGH (70% power) 1 minute; stir. Continue to microwave at 15-second intervals, stirring until morsels melt and mixture is smooth.
2. Whisk in corn syrup just until blended. Whisk in eggs just until blended. Add brown sugar and vanilla, whisking until blended. Stir in pecans. Spoon filling evenly into Cream Cheese Pastry shells.
3. Bake at 350° for 26 minutes or until crust is golden. Let cool in pans 5 minutes. Run a knife around outer edge of each pastry. Remove from pans, and let cool completely on wire racks (about 20 minutes).

Cream Cheese Pastry

Makes: 2 dozen • Hands-On Time: 20 min. • Total Time: 1 hr., 20 min.

½ cup butter, softened
½ (8-oz.) package cream cheese, softened
1¼ cups all-purpose flour

1. Beat butter and cream cheese at medium speed with an electric mixer until creamy. Gradually add flour to butter mixture, beating at low speed just until blended. Cover and chill dough 1 hour.
2. Shape dough into 24 (1¼-inch) balls, and place in cups of lightly greased miniature muffin pans; press dough to top of cups, forming shells. Cover loosely and chill until ready to use.

Make-Ahead Note: Make this pastry a day ahead, place it in miniature muffin pans and refrigerate overnight, if desired.

MAKE AHEAD
Hazelnut-Chocolate Mousse Tartlets

Makes: 3 dozen • Hands-On Time: 34 min. • Total Time: 3 hr., 24 min.

Smooth chocolate-hazelnut mousse is mounded in petite chocolate cookie crusts for tiny indulgences that are meant for a holiday tray.

⅓ cup hazelnuts
38 chocolate wafers, finely crushed
½ cup butter, melted
Paper or aluminum foil baking cups
8 (1-oz.) semisweet chocolate baking squares, coarsely chopped
2 cups heavy cream, divided
⅓ cup hazelnut spread
1 Tbsp. powdered sugar
Garnishes: sweetened whipped cream, chopped toasted hazelnuts

1. Preheat oven to 350°. Place nuts in a single layer in a shallow pan. Bake at 350° for 5 to 10 minutes or until skins begin to split. Transfer warm nuts to a colander; using a towel, rub briskly to remove skins. Pulse hazelnuts in a food processor 5 or 6 times or just until finely chopped. Add crushed wafers; pulse 1 or 2 times or until blended. Add melted butter; pulse 2 or 3 times or just until blended. Reduce oven temperature to 325°.
2. Place baking cups in 1 (24-cup) and 1 (12-cup) miniature muffin pans. Spoon about 1 Tbsp. crumb mixture into each cup. Press mixture into bottom and up sides of cups with back of a spoon. Bake at 325° for 7 minutes or just until set. Let cool completely (about 20 minutes).

3. Place chocolate and 1 cup whipping cream in a large microwave-safe bowl. Microwave at HIGH 1 minute; stir. Microwave 30 seconds; stir until smooth. Stir in hazelnut spread. Cover and chill 30 minutes or until slightly thickened.

4. Beat remaining 1 cup whipping cream and powdered sugar with an electric mixer until stiff peaks form; fold into chocolate mixture.

5. Spoon mousse mixture into a large decorating bag fitted with a metal star tip #1 C. Pipe mixture into prepared crusts. Cover and chill 2 to 8 hours. Garnish, if desired.

Note: We tested with Nutella hazelnut spread.

Make-Ahead Note: You can bake these chocolaty crusts, and freeze them up to 1 week in zip-top bags right in the pan. Then thaw and fill them as needed.

Fried Apricot Pies with Pecan Crust

Makes: 12 servings • Hands-On Time: 40 min. • Total Time: 2 hr., 40 min.

By using dried fruit in this recipe, these pies can be enjoyed any time of year. Serve them with butter pecan ice cream for a special treat.

    1 cup pecan halves
    3 Tbsp. sugar
    2 cups bread flour
    ½ tsp. salt
    ½ cup cold butter, cut into pieces
    1 large egg, beaten
    4 to 5 Tbsp. ice water
    1 cup dried apricots
    ⅓ cup sugar
    1 Tbsp. lemon juice
    ¼ tsp. ground cinnamon
    ⅛ tsp. ground nutmeg
       Vegetable oil
    ¼ cup sugar

1. Pulse pecans and 3 Tbsp. sugar in a food processor 10 to 15 times or until pecans are finely chopped. Add flour and salt; process 15 seconds. Add butter, and pulse 10 times or until mixture is crumbly. With processor running, pour beaten egg and ice water through food chute, processing just until dough forms a ball and leaves sides of bowl.

2. Shape dough into a disk. Wrap dough in wax paper; chill 1 hour or until ready to use.

3. Bring apricots and water to cover to a boil in a 2-quart saucepan over medium heat, and cook 30 minutes or until

very tender. Cool completely (about 30 minutes). Mash apricots, cooking liquid, ⅓ cup sugar, lemon juice, cinnamon, and nutmeg; set aside.

4. Divide dough into thirds. Roll 1 portion of dough to ⅛-inch thickness on a floured surface. Cut into 3 circles, using a 4½-inch round cutter. Spoon about 1 Tbsp. apricot mixture just below center of each dough circle. Fold dough over filling, pressing edges to seal. Crimp edges with a fork dipped in flour. Repeat with remaining dough and apricot mixture, rerolling dough scraps once.

5. Arrange pies in a single layer on a baking sheet; freeze 1 hour.

6. Pour oil to depth of 2 inches into a Dutch oven; heat to 375°. Fry pies, in batches, 2 minutes on each side or until golden brown. Drain on paper towels. Pour ¼ cup sugar into a shallow bowl. Dredge pies in sugar, turning to coat. Serve warm or at room temperature.

Double-Chocolate Chess Pie

Makes: 8 to 10 servings • Hands-On Time: 20 min. • Total Time: 2 hr., 5 min.

For a festive garnish, cut piecrust scraps into stars and bake at 350° for 5 to 7 minutes or until golden.

- 1½ cups firmly packed light brown sugar
- ¼ cup all-purpose flour
- 1½ Tbsp. unsweetened cocoa
- ½ (14.1-oz.) package refrigerated piecrusts
- 3 large eggs, lightly beaten
- 1 cup evaporated milk
- ⅓ cup butter, melted
- 2 oz. German chocolate baking squares, melted and cooled
- 2 Tbsp. light corn syrup
- 1 tsp. vanilla extract
- Garnishes: powdered sugar, whipped cream, chocolate curls

1. Preheat oven to 350°. Combine first 3 ingredients in a medium bowl.

2. Roll piecrust into a 13-inch circle on a flat surface. Fit into a 9-inch pie plate; fold edges under, and crimp. Whisk together eggs and next 5 ingredients in a large bowl. Gradually add sugar mixture, whisking until blended. Pour mixture into piecrust.

3. Bake at 350° for 45 minutes or until a knife inserted in center comes out almost clean. Let cool completely on a wire rack (about 1 hour). Sift powdered sugar over pie, or garnish, if desired.

White Chocolate-Peppermint Mousse Pie

Makes: 8 to 10 servings • Hands-On Time: 30 min. • Total Time: 8 hr., 30 min.

This make-ahead frozen dessert makes a perfect ending to a holiday meal.

24   cream-filled chocolate sandwich cookies, finely crushed
 6   Tbsp. butter, melted
 2   (4-oz.) white chocolate baking bars, chopped
 3   Tbsp. whipping cream
 ½   tsp. peppermint extract or 2 tsp. peppermint liqueur
 3   large egg whites
 ¾   cup sugar
12   drops red liquid food coloring
1½ cups whipping cream, whipped
Garnishes: frozen whipped topping, thawed; coarsely crushed hard peppermint candies

1. Stir together chocolate crumbs and melted butter; press firmly into an ungreased 9-inch deep-dish pie plate.

2. Microwave white chocolate in a microwave-safe bowl at HIGH 1 minute, stirring after 30 seconds. Microwave 3 Tbsp. whipping cream in a glass measuring cup at HIGH 30 seconds. Pour hot cream over white chocolate; let stand 1 minute. Stir until smooth. Stir in peppermint extract; cool 10 minutes.

3. Pour water to a depth of 1 inch into bottom of a double boiler over medium heat; bring to a boil. Reduce heat, and simmer; place egg whites and sugar in top of double boiler over simmering water. Cook, whisking constantly, 3 minutes or until sugar is dissolved. Beat egg white mixture over simmering water at medium speed with a handheld mixer until soft peaks form. Add food coloring. Increase speed to high, and beat until stiff peaks form. Fold in white chocolate mixture. Fold in whipped cream.

4. Spoon mousse mixture into prepared pie plate; cover and freeze 8 to 12 hours. Garnish, if desired.

Mini Apple-Cranberry Pies

Makes: 4 servings • Hands-On Time: 35 min.• Total Time: 3 hr., 5 min.

Classic apple pie takes on a new twist with the addition of cranberries in the filling that's laced with brandy.

2½ cups all-purpose flour
 1 Tbsp. brown sugar
 1 tsp. salt
 1 cup cold unsalted butter, cut up
 6 to 7 Tbsp. ice water
 ⅔ cup firmly packed brown sugar
 3 Tbsp. all-purpose flour
 ¼ tsp. apple pie spice
 6 cups sliced peeled Granny Smith apples (2¼ lb.)
1¼ cups sweetened dried cranberries
1½ Tbsp. brandy
 1 tsp. vanilla extract
 1 Tbsp. unsalted butter
 1 large egg, lightly beaten

1. Stir together first 3 ingredients in a large bowl. Cut in 1 cup butter with a pastry blender until mixture resembles small peas.

2. Mound flour mixture on 1 side of bowl. Drizzle 1 Tbsp. ice water along edge of mixture in bowl. Using a fork, gently toss a small amount of flour mixture into water just until dry ingredients are moistened. Move mixture to other side of bowl, and repeat procedure with remaining ice water, 1 Tbsp. at a time, until a dough forms.

3. Gently gather dough into 2 flat disks. Wrap in plastic wrap, and chill 45 minutes.

4. Roll 1 dough disk to ⅛-inch thickness; cut into 4 (7-inch) circles. Fit 1 circle into each of 4 (4½-inch) pie plates. Chill 15 minutes.

5. Meanwhile, preheat oven to 425°. Combine ⅔ cup brown sugar and next 2 ingredients; stir in apples and next 3 ingredients. Spoon about 1¾ cups apple mixture into each crust, packing tightly and mounding in center; dot pies with 1 Tbsp. butter cut into pieces.

6. Roll remaining dough disk to ⅛-inch thickness. For double-crust pies, cut dough into 2 (7-inch) circles. Gently place 1 circle over filling in each pie; fold edges under, and crimp, sealing to bottom crust. Cut slits or a hole in top of pies for steam to escape. Brush dough with beaten egg. For lattice-topped pies, cut dough into ½-inch-wide strips. Arrange strips in a lattice design over filling; fold excess bottom pie crust under and along edges of top pie crust. Gently press ends of strips, sealing bottom pie crust. Brush lattice with beaten egg. Place pies on a large baking sheet.

7. Bake at 425° for 30 minutes or until crust is golden brown. Transfer to a wire rack, and cool 1 hour before serving.

Caramel-Pumpkin Pie with Caramel Sauce

Makes: 8 servings • Hands-On Time: 21 min. • Total Time: 3 hr., 10 min., including dough

To save time, substitute a refrigerated piecrust.

Buttery Pastry Dough
All-purpose flour
2 cups sugar
2 Tbsp. light corn syrup
1½ cups heavy cream, divided
2 Tbsp. butter
1 (15-oz.) can pumpkin
4 large eggs, lightly beaten
¼ cup butter, melted
1½ tsp. pumpkin pie spice
½ tsp. salt
Sweetened whipped cream

1. Place Buttery Pastry Dough disk on a lightly floured surface; sprinkle dough lightly with flour. Roll dough to ⅛-inch thickness. Starting at 1 edge of dough, wrap dough around a rolling pin. Place rolling pin over a 9-inch pie plate, and unroll dough over pie plate. Trim off excess dough along edges; crimp edges. Cover and chill.
2. Preheat oven to 350°. Combine sugar, corn syrup, and ¼ cup water in a 3-qt. heavy saucepan, stirring until sugar dissolves. Bring to a boil over medium heat, without stirring. Cook 18 minutes or until mixture is amber colored, swirling pan to incorporate mixture (do not stir).
3. Remove from heat; quickly stir in 1 cup cream and 2 Tbsp. butter. Cook over medium heat, stirring constantly, until caramel is smooth (about 1 minute). Stir in remaining ½ cup cream. Let cool 10 minutes.
4. Whisk together pumpkin and next 4 ingredients until blended. Gradually whisk in 1½ cups caramel mixture. Pour into prepared crust.
5. Bake at 350° for 40 to 45 minutes or just until center is set. Let cool completely on a wire rack (about 1 hour). Serve with sweetened whipped cream and remaining caramel sauce.

Buttery Pastry Dough

Makes: enough for 1 (9-inch) piecrust • Hands-On Time: 10 min. • Total Time: 40 min.

1¼ cups all-purpose flour
¼ tsp. salt
¼ cup cold butter, cut up
¼ cup cold shortening, cut up
2 Tbsp. ice water

1. Pulse flour and salt in a food processor 2 or 3 times or until blended. Add butter and shortening; pulse until mixture is crumbly. Add ice water, 1 Tbsp. at a time, and pulse until mixture holds together when pressed. Shape into a flat disk; wrap in plastic wrap, and chill 30 minutes.

EDITOR'S FAVORITE
Chocolate Chip Black Bottom Fudge Pie

Makes: 10 servings • Hands-On Time: 10 min. • Total Time: 1 hr., 10 min.

A puddle of chocolate fudge rests between the crust and filling of this rich dessert.

½ (14.1-oz.) package refrigerated piecrusts
2 cups semisweet chocolate morsels, divided
2 Tbsp. whipping cream
1 cup butter, melted
½ cup granulated sugar
½ cup firmly packed brown sugar
½ cup all-purpose flour
2 tsp. vanilla extract or vanilla bean paste
¼ tsp. salt
2 large eggs
1 cup coarsely chopped toasted pecans
Vanilla ice cream

1. Preheat oven to 325°. Unroll piecrust, and fit into a 9-inch deep-dish pie plate; fold edges under, and crimp. Microwave 1 cup chocolate morsels and whipping cream in a medium microwave-safe bowl at HIGH 45 seconds to 1½ minutes; stir until smooth. Spread melted chocolate over crust.
2. Whisk together butter and next 6 ingredients in a large bowl until well blended. Stir in remaining 1 cup chocolate morsels and pecans. Pour filling over chocolate in crust.
3. Bake at 325° for 1 hour or just until set. Cool completely. Serve with ice cream.

Homemade
PIZZA PARTY

AFTER A LONG DAY OF CHRISTMAS
SHOPPING, BRING THE PIZZA PARLOR
TO YOUR HOME, AND SERVE UP A
SLICE OF PIE THE WHOLE
FAMILY WILL LOVE.

The Farmer's Pizza

Makes: 8 servings • Hands-On Time: 10 min. • Total Time: 1 hr., 20 min.

What makes this pizza great are the farm-fresh ingredients.

- 2 oz. thinly sliced pancetta
- 1 cup thinly sliced sweet onion
- 1 recipe Sourdough Pizza Dough
- 1 Tbsp. olive oil
- 1 cup Spicy Tomato Pizza Sauce (page 114)
- 1 cup cherry tomatoes, halved
- ½ cup mascarpone cheese, softened and divided
- 2 cups packed arugula leaves

1. Cook pancetta in a large skillet over medium-high heat 3 minutes or until cooked but not crisp, turning often. Drain on paper towels, reserving drippings in skillet. Cook onion in hot drippings, stirring often, 5 minutes or until tender.
2. Stretch pizza dough into a 12-inch circle on a lightly floured surface. (No need to perfect the round shape.) Place on a lightly floured baking sheet. Brush olive oil over dough using a pastry brush. (If you don't have a pastry brush, drizzle oil evenly over dough.) Cover loosely with plastic wrap, and let rise in a warm place (85°), free from drafts, 20 to 25 minutes.
3. Place a pizza stone or baking sheet in oven. Preheat oven to 450° for 30 minutes. Remove and discard plastic wrap from dough. Slide dough from baking sheet onto hot pizza stone or baking sheet in oven. Bake at 450° for 5 minutes.
4. Spread pizza sauce over partially baked crust, leaving a 1-inch border. Top with tomatoes, pancetta, and onion. Dollop ¼ cup cheese by rounded tablespoonfuls over pizza.
5. Bake at 450° for 15 minutes or until crust is golden. Immediately dollop remaining cheese over pizza. Sprinkle with arugula.

Sourdough Pizza Dough

Makes: 1 (12-inch) dough portion • Hands-On Time: 6 min. • Total Time: 12 hr., 21 min. plus 1 day for starter

- 1½ cups Sourdough Primary Batter
- 1½ cups all-purpose flour
- 1½ tsp. kosher salt
- 2 Tbsp. extra virgin olive oil

1. Combine all ingredients in bowl of a heavy-duty electric stand mixer. Beat at low speed until smooth and blended. Beat at medium speed 1 minute.
2. Turn dough out onto a well-floured surface, and knead until

smooth and elastic (about 4 to 6 minutes, sprinkling surface with flour as needed).
3. Place dough in a greased bowl, turning to grease the top. Cover with plastic wrap; let rise in a warm place (85°), free from drafts, 1 to 1½ hours or until doubled in bulk and dough is springy when lightly touched. Punch dough down, and shape according to directions in desired recipe.

Sourdough Primary Batter

Makes: about 2 cups • Hands-On Time: 10 min. • Total Time: 8 hr., 10 min.

- 1 cup Sourdough Starter
- 1 cup warm water (85°)
- 1½ cups all-purpose flour

1. Place 1 cup Sourdough Starter in a large warm bowl. Cover remaining starter, and return to refrigerator. Stir warm water (85°) into starter in bowl. Add flour, ½ cup at a time, stirring well after each addition. Cover and place in a warm place (85°), free from drafts, 8 to 10 hours. Batter should have many large bubbles and have a yeasty, slightly sour yet pleasant odor, when it is ready to use. Measure out 1½ cups Sourdough Primary Batter for Sourdough Pizza Dough, returning remaining batter (at least 1 cup) to Sourdough Starter in refrigerator. Store covered in coldest part of refrigerator. (This feeds the starter to keep it going.)

Note: Repeat this procedure for use in future recipes. (Always remember to return at least 1 cup batter to starter before preparing a recipe.) Sourdough Starter can be maintained in this manner indefinitely. Always remove starter from storage container and wash container well with each use. Return starter to clean container.

Sourdough Starter

Makes: about 2 cups • Hands-On Time: 10 min. • Total Time: 10 hr., 15 min.

- 1 (¼-oz.) envelope active dry yeast
- 1 Tbsp. sugar
- 2 cups warm water (100° to 110°), divided
- 2 cups all-purpose flour

1. Dissolve yeast and sugar in 1 cup warm water in a medium-size glass bowl, stirring well. Let stand 5 minutes or until bubbly. Gradually add remaining warm water and flour; mix well using a wooden spoon. Cover with plastic wrap, and let stand in a warm place (85°), free from drafts, 10 to 12 hours. Label fermented mixture, and store in refrigerator. Stir daily; use within 11 days to prepare Sourdough Primary Batter.

Mini Pesto Pizzas with Zucchini Ribbons, Fontina, and Eggs

Makes: 4 servings • Hands-On Time: 15 min. • Total Time: 37 min., including pesto

Make an indentation in the melted cheese with the back of a spoon to create a "nest" for the broken egg.

1 recipe Sourdough Pizza Dough (page 111)
2 Tbsp. olive oil
Basil-Mint Pesto
1 cup (4 oz.) shredded fontina cheese
1 medium zucchini, halved lengthwise
4 large eggs
Salt and freshly ground pepper to taste
Fresh basil leaves

1. Preheat oven to 500°. Shape dough into 4 (4-inch) rounds on a lightly greased baking sheet. Brush dough rounds with olive oil. Spread rounds evenly with Basil-Mint Pesto; sprinkle with cheese.
2. Cut zucchini lengthwise into thin ribbons using a vegetable peeler. Arrange zucchini evenly on pizzas. Make a well in center of each pizza.
3. Bake at 500° for 7 minutes or just until edges begin to brown. Break 1 egg onto center of each pizza. Bake 7 more minutes or to desired degree of doneness. Just before serving, season with salt and pepper to taste; top with basil.

Basil-Mint Pesto

Makes: about ¾ cup • Hands-On Time: 8 min. • Total Time: 8 min.

1½   cups loosely packed fresh basil leaves
½   cup loosely packed fresh mint leaves
⅓   cup grated Asiago or Parmesan cheese
¼   cup extra virgin olive oil
¼   cup pine nuts, toasted
1   tsp. lemon juice
¼   tsp. salt
¼   tsp. freshly ground pepper
¼   tsp. dried crushed red pepper
3   garlic cloves

1. Process all ingredients in a food processor until smooth, stopping to scrape down sides as needed.

Pear, Hazelnut, and Gouda Pizzas

(pictured on page 116)
Makes: 6 servings • Hands-On Time: 15 min. • Total Time: 21 min.

If you're short on time, buy a favorite bottled vinaigrette to toss with the salad greens.

Vegetable cooking spray
Whole Wheat Pizza Dough
Parchment paper
¼   cup hazelnut oil or olive oil, divided
1½   cups shredded smoked Gouda cheese
2   ripe Bosc pears, thinly sliced
1   Tbsp. balsamic vinegar
1   Tbsp. finely chopped shallot
1½   tsp. honey
⅛   tsp. salt
⅛   tsp. freshly ground pepper
3   cups loosely packed gourmet mixed salad greens
⅔   cup toasted hazelnuts, coarsely chopped

1. Coat cold cooking grate of grill with cooking spray, and place on grill. Preheat grill to 350° (medium heat).
2. Divide pizza dough into 6 equal portions. Roll 1 portion of dough at a time into a 6-inch round on a lightly floured surface. Transfer dough rounds to a parchment paper-lined baking sheet. Brush dough with 1 Tbsp. hazelnut oil.
3. Slide pizza dough rounds off baking sheet; flip dough over onto cooking grate of grill. Grill, covered with grill lid, 2 minutes. Brush tops with 1 Tbsp. hazelnut oil. Flip pizzas, and top evenly with cheese and pear slices. Grill 3 more minutes or until crusts are golden brown and cheese is melted.

4. Whisk together vinegar, next 4 ingredients, and remaining 2 Tbsp. hazelnut oil in a bowl. Add salad greens; toss to coat. Top each pizza with about ½ cup salad greens. Sprinkle with hazelnuts.
Note: Work quickly to top each pizza with cheese and pear slices while pizzas are on the grill. We recommend using spring-loaded tongs.

Whole Wheat Pizza Dough

Makes: 1 (12-inch) dough portion • Hands-On Time: 12 min. • Total Time: 1 hr., 22 min.

This pizza dough can be made a day ahead. After allowing the dough to rise, punch it down and refrigerate it overnight. Allow the dough to come to room temperature before using.

1¼   tsp. active dry yeast
⅔   cup warm water (100° to 110°)
1   cup all-purpose flour
¾   cup whole wheat flour
1½   tsp. sea salt
1   tsp. honey
2   to 3 tsp. extra virgin olive oil

1. Combine yeast and warm water in bowl of a heavy-duty electric stand mixer. Let stand 5 minutes or until foamy. Add all-purpose flour and next 2 ingredients to yeast mixture; beat at low speed (using a dough hook attachment) until smooth and blended. Add honey and 2 tsp. olive oil; beat at low speed 2 minutes. Gradually add remaining 1 tsp. olive oil if needed to make a soft dough. Beat at medium speed 4 minutes or until dough forms a ball and pulls away from sides of bowl. Knead dough on a well-floured surface until smooth and elastic (about 5 minutes). (Dough should be slightly sticky.)
2. Place dough in a well-greased bowl, turning to grease top. Cover dough with plastic wrap, and let rise in a warm place (85°), free from drafts, 1 hour or until doubled in bulk.
3. Punch dough down; let stand 5 minutes. Shape into a ball.

FIX IT FASTER

Short on time? Pick up a pound of prepared pizza dough from the bakery at your local grocery store and swap it for any of the recipes in this chapter. You may also use the Sourdough Pizza Dough or Whole Wheat Pizza Dough interchangeably.

Gorgonzola, Prosciutto, and Date Pizza

(pictured on page 116)

Makes: 8 to 10 servings • Hands-On Time: 12 min. • Total Time: 40 min.

Wow your crowd with this decadent white pizza featuring caramelized sherried shallots and sweet Medjool dates.

- 1   recipe Whole Wheat Pizza Dough (page 113)
Cornmeal
- 1   cup sliced shallots (4 large)
- 1   Tbsp. olive oil, divided
- 2   tsp. sherry vinegar
- ⅓   cup refrigerated Alfredo sauce
- ⅔   cup crumbled Gorgonzola cheese
- ½   cup chopped dried Medjool dates
- 2   oz. thinly sliced prosciutto, cut crosswise into ½-inch pieces
- ½   tsp. fresh rosemary leaves
- ⅓   cup whole Marcona almonds, toasted

1. Preheat oven to 450°. Heat pizza stone according to manufacturer's instructions. Roll dough into a 12-inch circle on a lightly floured surface. Sprinkle cornmeal on preheated stone; place dough on stone. Bake at 450° for 13 minutes.

2. Sauté shallots in 1 Tbsp. hot oil in a nonstick skillet over medium heat 10 minutes or until tender. Add sherry vinegar and cook 2 more minutes or until vinegar is absorbed.

3. Spread Alfredo sauce evenly on pizza dough, leaving a ½-inch border. Top with sautéed shallots, Gorgonzola cheese, dates, and prosciutto. Sprinkle with rosemary.

4. Bake at 450° for 15 minutes or until crust is golden and cheese is bubbly. Sprinkle with toasted almonds. Let stand 5 minutes before serving.

Carne Lover's Pizza

(pictured on page 116)

Makes: 8 servings • Hands-On Time: 10 min. • Total Time: 2 hr., 12 min.

- 1   recipe Sourdough Pizza Dough (page 111)
- 1   medium-size yellow onion, cut vertically into thin slices
- 1   lb. mild Italian pork sausage, casings removed
- 2   Tbsp. olive oil
- 6   (1-oz.) mozzarella cheese slices
- 6   cooked bacon slices, crumbled
- 2   oz. thin pepperoni slices (about 28 slices)
- ½   cup chopped Canadian bacon slices (5 slices)
- 1½ cups Spicy Tomato Pizza Sauce

1. Let pizza dough stand, covered, at room temperature 1 hour.

2. Meanwhile, cook onion and sausage in a large skillet over medium-high heat, stirring often, 8 minutes or until sausage crumbles and is no longer pink; drain.

3. Brush a 12-inch cast-iron skillet with oil. Press dough on bottom and up sides of skillet. Cover dough loosely with plastic wrap, and let rise in a warm place (85°), free from drafts, 30 minutes. Press dough up sides of skillet.

4. Preheat oven to 450°. Bake pizza at 450° for 6 minutes or until crust is set and beginning to brown. Remove skillet from oven. Lay cheese slices on top of crust, slightly overlapping. Layer sausage mixture, bacon, pepperoni, and Canadian bacon over cheese. Spread pizza sauce over meats.

5. Bake at 450° for 18 to 20 minutes or until crust is golden.

Spicy Tomato Pizza Sauce

Makes: 2 cups • Hands-On Time: 5 min. • Total Time: 30 min.

This recipe makes enough sauce for two pizzas. Store any remaining sauce in an airtight container in the refrigerator for up to one week.

- 1   (28-oz.) can whole tomatoes
- 2   garlic cloves, minced
- 2   Tbsp. olive oil
- 1   Tbsp. chopped fresh basil
- 1   Tbsp. chopped fresh oregano
- ½   tsp. kosher salt
- ¼   tsp. freshly ground pepper
- ½   tsp. dried crushed red pepper

1. Crush tomatoes with a fork or with your hands, reserving juices.

2. Sauté garlic in hot oil in a medium saucepan 1 minute over medium heat. Add tomatoes with juice, basil and next 4 ingredients; bring to a boil. Reduce heat, and simmer 20 to 25 minutes, stirring frequently, until sauce is reduced to 2 cups.

Note: We tested with San Marzano tomatoes, the best quality canned tomato product available. Find them online or in cook stores.

Note: Dried crushed red pepper is a classic ingredient in pizza sauce. If kids are involved in the eating, feel free to decrease or omit it.

Barbecued Pork and Pineapple Pizza

Makes: 8 servings • Hands-On Time: 25 min. • Total Time: 1 hr., 43 min.

Slow-cooked pork gives this Hawaiian-style pizza a dash of Southern flare.

- 1 recipe Whole Wheat Pizza Dough (page 113)
- 2 Tbsp. olive oil, divided
- 1 large red onion, thinly sliced and separated into rings
- ½ cup barbecue sauce
- 1 cup shredded barbecued pork
- ½ cup chopped fresh pineapple
- 1 cup shredded smoked Gouda cheese
- 1 cup (4 oz.) shredded fontina cheese
- ¼ cup chopped fresh cilantro

1. Preheat oven to 450°. Let pizza dough stand at room temperature 1 to 2 hours. Brush a jelly-roll pan with 1 Tbsp. olive oil. Stretch dough into a 14-inch circle on pan.
2. Sauté onion in remaining 1 Tbsp. hot oil in a large nonstick skillet over medium-high heat 10 to 15 minutes or until tender.
3. Spread barbecue sauce on pizza dough, leaving a ½-inch border. Top with shredded pork, pineapple, and sautéed onion. Sprinkle with cheeses.
4. Bake at 450° for 18 to 20 minutes or until crust is golden. Sprinkle with cilantro.

Carne Lover's Pizza

Sweet Potato-Brie Pizza

Pear, Hazelnut, and Gouda Pizzas

Gorgonzola, Prosciutto, and Date Pizza

Sweet Potato-Brie Pizza

(pictured on facing page)
Makes: 6 servings • Hands-On Time: 8 min. • Total Time: 38 min.

This pizza can also be made into a round. Use the herbs you have on hand. We recommend 1 Tbsp. chopped rosemary as a substitute for the sage.

- 3 Tbsp. garlic-flavored olive oil, divided
- 1 recipe Whole Wheat Pizza Dough (page 113)
- 1 medium-size sweet potato (about 8 oz.), peeled
- 1 Fuji apple, thinly sliced
- 2 shallots, sliced
- ¼ tsp. freshly ground pepper
- ¼ cup firmly packed brown sugar
- 1 (8-oz.) Brie round, cut into ½-inch cubes
- 10 small fresh sage leaves

1. Preheat oven to 450°. Brush a 15- x 10-inch jelly-roll pan with 1 Tbsp. olive oil. Stretch dough into a 15- x 10-inch rectangle on pan. Brush 1 Tbsp. olive oil on dough.
2. Thinly slice sweet potato crosswise. Toss sweet potato, apple, shallots, and remaining 1 Tbsp. olive oil in a bowl. Arrange sweet potato, apple, and shallots over dough. Sprinkle with pepper.
3. Bake at 450° for 20 minutes or until edges are golden and potatoes and apples are slightly cooked. Remove from oven; sprinkle with brown sugar, and top with cheese. Bake 10 more minutes or until cheese is melted. Sprinkle with sage leaves.

Note: For appetizer servings, lift this large uncut pizza onto a cutting board, and cut it into small wedges using a pizza wheel.

KIDS IN THE KITCHEN

Gather the whole family together and create your own Italian masterpieces. Divide each dough round into 4 pieces, slather on your favorite sauce, and sprinkle with your favorite toppings.

Mushroom and Caramelized Onion Pizza

Makes: 4 to 6 servings • Hands-On Time: 29 min. • Total Time: 41 min.

Be sure to preheat your baking stone according to the manufacturer's instructions to ensure a crispy crust.

- 1 large sweet onion, cut into ¼-inch slices
- 2 Tbsp. olive oil, divided
- 2 Tbsp. butter, divided
- 1½ Tbsp. balsamic vinegar
- 1 (8-oz.) package baby portobello mushrooms, sliced
- ½ tsp. salt
- ¼ tsp. freshly ground pepper
- 2 large garlic cloves, minced
- 1 Tbsp. chopped fresh oregano
- 1 Tbsp. chopped fresh thyme
- 1 recipe Sourdough Pizza Dough (page 111)
- 1 Tbsp. yellow cornmeal
- 1½ (8-oz.) blocks mozzarella cheese, shredded and divided
- ¼ cup (1-oz.) shredded Parmesan cheese

1. Preheat oven to 450°. Heat pizza stone according to manufacturer's instructions.
2. Separate onion slices into rings. Heat 1 Tbsp. oil and 1 Tbsp. butter in a large nonstick skillet over medium heat until butter melts. Add onion, and cook 15 minutes or until onion is caramelized, stirring occasionally. Stir in balsamic vinegar, and cook, stirring constantly, 2 minutes. Remove from heat.
3. Meanwhile, heat remaining 1 Tbsp. oil and 1 Tbsp. butter in a large skillet over medium-high heat until butter melts. Add mushrooms and next 3 ingredients. Cook until mushrooms are browned and liquid evaporates, stirring occasionally. Remove from heat; stir in oregano and thyme.
4. Roll dough into a 12-inch circle on a lightly floured surface. Sprinkle cornmeal on preheated stone; place dough on stone. Bake at 450° for 10 minutes.
5. Sprinkle 1 cup mozzarella cheese on pizza crust; top with onion and mushroom mixtures. Sprinkle remaining 2 cups mozzarella cheese and Parmesan cheese over vegetables. Bake 5 more minutes or until crust is golden brown and cheese melts.

Note: Pizza may be baked on a large baking sheet. Do not preheat baking sheet in oven.

Make-Ahead APPETIZERS

HOSTING A HOLIDAY PARTY IS EASY WHEN YOU HAVE THIS REPERTOIRE OF DELICIOUS MAKE-AHEAD MEAL STARTERS.

Celery Root Latkes with Caramelized Apple Purée

Makes: 3½ dozen • Hands-On Time: 1 hr., 20 min. • Total Time: 1 hr., 20 min.

Inspired by traditional potato latkes, these petite pancakes are made with a blend of starch-heavy baking potatoes and celery root (also known as celeriac) for an added twist of flavor, then topped with caramelized apple purée and a dollop of crème fraîche. Latkes can be made ahead of time. Cool completely, then layer between sheets of wax paper in an airtight container, and chill or freeze. Reheat in a 375° oven for 10 minutes or until crisp. Caramelized apple purée can be made several days ahead of time and stored in the refrigerator or freezer.

2   Tbsp. butter
4   Gala apples (about 2 lb.), peeled and coarsely chopped
2   Tbsp. sugar
2   Tbsp. apple cider
2   small baking potatoes (about 1 lb.)
1   small yellow onion
1   medium celery root (about ¾ lb.)
⅓   cup all-purpose flour
¾   tsp. kosher salt
¼   tsp. freshly ground pepper
1   large egg, lightly beaten
½   cup vegetable oil
6   Tbsp. crème fraîche
Garnish: watercress leaves

1. Melt butter in a large skillet over medium heat. Add apple to skillet; sprinkle with sugar. Stir in apple cider, and cook 15 minutes or until apples are tender and caramelized, stirring occasionally. Process apple mixture in a food processor until smooth. Transfer to a small bowl. Cool completely; cover and chill until ready to serve.
2. Shred potatoes using the large holes of a box grater. Transfer shredded potatoes to a large bowl of cold water. Drain potatoes. Grate onion. Place potato and onion in a kitchen towel; squeeze out excess liquid. Transfer potato mixture to a large bowl.
3. Coarsely grate celery root; add to potato mixture. Stir in flour and next 3 ingredients.
4. Heat oil in a large nonstick skillet over medium heat. Spoon about 2 Tbsp. batter for each latke into skillet. Cook latkes 3 minutes or until golden brown and edges look cooked. Turn and cook other side. Drain on paper towels. Arrange latkes in a single layer on a serving platter. Top each latke with 1 dollop each of caramelized apple and crème fraîche. Garnish, if desired.

Rosemary-Red Wine Wafers

Makes: 5 dozen • Hands-On Time: 18 min. • Total Time: 4 hr., 33 min.

These simple crackers get a flavor boost from red wine, rosemary, and fresh black pepper. We recommend serving them with an assortment of cheeses, fruit pastes, or chutneys. The dough can be refrigerated for up to two days or stored in the freezer for up to a month.

1½ cups all-purpose flour
2   tsp. coarsely ground black pepper
2   tsp. chopped fresh rosemary
1   tsp. coarse sea salt, divided
½   cup unsalted butter, cut into pieces
5   to 6 Tbsp. dry red wine

1. Pulse flour, pepper, rosemary, and ½ tsp. sea salt in a food processor 5 times or just until blended. Add butter; pulse just until mixture is crumbly.
2. With processor running, gradually add red wine through food chute, 1 Tbsp. at a time, and process until dough forms a ball and leaves sides of bowl. Shape dough into an 8- x 2-inch log; wrap in plastic wrap, and refrigerate 3 to 8 hours.
3. Preheat oven to 325°. Cut log into ⅛-inch-thick rounds; place rounds on parchment paper-lined baking sheet. Sprinkle evenly with remaining ½ tsp. salt.
4. Bake at 325° for 25 to 30 minutes or until golden brown. Let cool 5 minutes on baking sheet; remove to a wire rack, and cool completely (about 15 minutes). Store in an airtight container up to 5 days.

DECK THE BAR

Having a crowd over for a holiday open house? Set up a decorative display designated for the bar area. Festive martini, high ball, and wine glasses allow guests to make their own cocktails. Don't forget to include bowls of limes, lemons, olives, and maraschino cherries. And, add a tall shooter glass full of colorful swizzle sticks to make the tray complete.

MAKE AHEAD
Carrot-Ginger Soup Shots

Makes: 3 cups • Hands-On Time: 22 min. • Total Time: 1 hr., 5 min.

Serve this fragrant golden soup in shot glasses on a tray at your next holiday party. It's good warm or chilled (see box).

   2   tsp. butter
   1   tsp. olive oil
   1   cup chopped red onion
   1   Tbsp. grated fresh ginger
   3   garlic cloves, minced
   3   cups vegetable broth
   2   cups chopped carrots (about 5 carrots)
   ¼   cup fresh orange juice
   ⅛   tsp. salt
   ¼   cup half-and-half (optional)
   Garnishes: plain yogurt or sour cream, chives

1. Melt butter with oil in a large saucepan over medium heat; add onion, and cook, stirring often, 5 minutes or until almost tender. Add ginger and garlic; cook, stirring often, 3 minutes. Add broth and carrots.
2. Bring to a boil; reduce heat, and simmer 25 minutes or until carrots are very tender. Stir in orange juice and salt. Remove from heat; let cool 10 minutes. Stir in half-and-half, if desired.
3. Process soup in a blender until smooth, stopping to scrape down sides as needed. Garnish, if desired.

Carrot-Ginger Soup Shots

SOUP'S ON!

To Serve Warm: Divide soup among shot glasses (about 2 Tbsp. each). Top each serving with ⅛ tsp. yogurt or thinned sour cream. Drag a wooden pick through the center of yogurt several times to swirl, if desired.

To Serve Cold: Cover and chill soup 2 to 24 hours. Whisk soup, and carefully divide among shot glasses (about 2 Tbsp. each). Top each serving with ⅛ tsp. yogurt or thinned sour cream. Drag a wooden pick through the center of yogurt several times to swirl, if desired.

MAKE AHEAD
Wishing Star Cheese Crackers

Makes: 3 dozen • Hands-On Time: 20 min. • Total Time: 2 hr., 55 min.

These little cheese crackers will remind you of your child's favorite fish-shaped snack cracker. For Christmas, make these fun, cheesy crackers for the young and the young at heart.

   1   cup all-purpose flour
   ¾   tsp. salt
   ¼   cup cold butter, cut into pieces
   1½   cups (6 oz.) Colby Jack cheese, shredded
   ¼   cup ice water
   Parchment paper

1. Pulse flour and salt in a food processor just until blended. Add butter, and pulse 7 times or just until mixture is crumbly. Add cheese, and pulse 7 times or just until mixture again is crumbly.
2. Gradually add enough water, 1 Tbsp. at a time, through food chute, pulsing just until mixture forms a ball. Shape dough into a disk. Wrap dough in plastic wrap; chill 2 hours.
3. Preheat oven to 350°. Roll dough between 2 sheets of parchment paper to ⅛-inch thickness. Cut into star shapes using a 2-inch cutter.
4. Place crackers on parchment paper-lined baking sheets. Bake at 350° for 15 minutes or until puffed and golden. Remove from baking sheet, and let cool completely on a wire rack.

MAKE AHEAD
Cranberry Salsa

Makes: 2½ cups • Hands-On Time: 8 min. • Total Time: 2 hr., 8 min.

Jalapeño fires up the flavor of this pretty appetizer. Serve it with sweet potato chips or cinnamon sugar pita chips.

2 cups fresh or frozen cranberries, thawed
1 small Gala, Fuji, or Braeburn apple, cubed
1 medium-size jalapeño pepper, seeded and quartered
1 green onion, finely chopped
2 Tbsp. chopped fresh cilantro (optional)
¼ cup superfine sugar
1 Tbsp. fresh lime juice
1 Tbsp. canola oil
½ tsp. salt

1. Pulse first 3 ingredients in a food processor 4 times or just until coarsely chopped, stopping to scrape down sides as needed. Transfer to a bowl; stir in green onion and, if desired, cilantro.
2. Add sugar and remaining 3 ingredients, stirring well. Cover and chill 2 to 24 hours. Stir before serving.

MAKE AHEAD
Lemony Feta Dip with Oven-Roasted Tomatoes

Makes: 8 servings • Hands-On Time: 15 min. • Total Time: 45 min.

All your favorite flavors of a Greek salad–in a dip! It's a great way to present Mediterranean flavors.

4 plum tomatoes, halved lengthwise and seeded
¼ cup extra virgin olive oil, divided
¼ tsp. salt
½ tsp. freshly ground black pepper, divided
3 garlic cloves
3 (4-oz.) containers crumbled feta cheese
1 tsp. lemon zest
1½ Tbsp. lemon juice
2 Tbsp. chopped fresh oregano
Garnishes: additional extra virgin olive oil, fresh oregano leaves, chopped kalamata olives
Pita wedges or pita chips

1. Preheat oven to 450°. Place tomato halves, cut sides up, on a jelly-roll pan. Drizzle with 2 Tbsp. olive oil, and sprinkle with salt and ¼ tsp. pepper.

Cranberry Salsa

2. Bake at 450° for 30 minutes or until tomato halves are tender and caramelized. Remove tomato halves from oven, cool, and cut into bite-sized pieces.
3. With processor running, drop garlic through food chute; process until minced. Add cheese, lemon zest, lemon juice, chopped oregano, remaining 2 Tbsp. oil, and remaining ¼ tsp. pepper. Process until smooth. Spoon dip into a bowl. Top with tomato, and garnish, if desired. Serve with pita wedges or chips.

Tip: If making dip ahead of time, top with tomato just before serving.

Barbecued Pork Tartlets with Slaw Topping

Makes: 24 tartlets • Hands-On Time: 30 min. • Total Time: 1 hr., 5 min.

These savory appetizers can be dressed up or down depending on your occasion. Make the slaw ahead; stir in the radishes at the last minute to prevent discoloring the slaw.

¼ cup mayonnaise
1 Tbsp. white vinegar
1 tsp. whole grain mustard
¼ tsp. salt
¼ tsp. freshly ground pepper
2 cups packed angel hair slaw, finely chopped
3 radishes, thinly sliced
¾ lb. shredded barbecued pork without sauce, chopped
¾ cup barbecue sauce
¼ cup chopped green onions
1 (14.1-oz.) package refrigerated piecrusts

1. Preheat oven to 350°. Whisk together first 5 ingredients in a medium bowl. Stir in slaw and radishes. Cover and chill, if desired.
2. Stir together pork and next 2 ingredients.
3. Unroll 1 piecrust on a flat surface. Cut into 12 rounds, using a 2-inch round cutter. Press rounds into 12 cups of a lightly greased 24-cup miniature muffin pan. (Dough will come slightly up sides, forming a cup.) Repeat procedure with remaining piecrust, pressing rounds into remaining 12 cups of muffin pan. Spoon 1 rounded Tbsp. pork mixture into each cup.
4. Bake at 350° for 35 minutes or until edges of dough are lightly browned. Remove from pans. Top with slaw.

Sweet Potato, Cheddar, and Chive Biscuits with Country Ham

Makes: 3 dozen • Hands-On Time: 25 min. • Total Time: 50 min.

Make this dough the day before a big party, and all you have to do is pop the biscuits in the oven just before guests arrive. Smear them with a favorite herbed butter or apple butter, and tuck in slivers of ham.

- 2¾ cups all-purpose flour
- 1 Tbsp. sugar
- 1 Tbsp. baking powder
- 1½ tsp. salt
- 1½ tsp. freshly ground pepper
- ¼ cup cold butter, cut into pieces
- 1 cup (4 oz.) freshly shredded extra-sharp Cheddar cheese
- ¼ cup chopped fresh chives
- 1 cup cooked, mashed sweet potatoes
- ⅓ cup buttermilk
- 2 large eggs
  Parchment paper
- 2 Tbsp. butter, melted
- ½ lb. thinly sliced country ham

1. Preheat oven to 375°. Stir together first 5 ingredients in a large bowl; cut in ¼ cup butter with a pastry blender until mixture resembles small peas and dough is crumbly. Stir in cheese and chives.

2. Stir together sweet potatoes, buttermilk, and eggs. Add to flour mixture, stirring just until dry ingredients are moistened.

3. Turn dough out onto a lightly floured surface. Pat dough into a 1-inch-thick circle. Cut dough with a well-floured 1½-inch round cutter, rerolling scraps as needed.

4. Line baking sheet with parchment paper; place biscuits, with sides touching, on prepared baking sheet. Brush tops with 2 Tbsp. melted butter.

5. Bake at 375° for 25 minutes or until golden brown.

6. Cook ham in a large nonstick skillet over medium-high heat 6 minutes, turning once. Split biscuits; fill with ham.

Make-Ahead Note: Wrap and freeze dough cutouts overnight. Remove from freezer; place on parchment paper-lined baking sheet. Bake at 375° for 28 minutes or until golden brown.

Sweet Potato, Cheddar, and Chive Biscuits with Country Ham

Bacon-Wrapped Blue Cheese Dates

Makes: 36 appetizer servings • Hands-On Time: 24 min. • Total Time: 45 min.

- ¼ cup chopped pecans
- 18 bacon slices
- ½ cup crumbled blue cheese
- ¼ cup softened cream cheese
- 36 medium-size pitted dates
  Wooden picks

1. Preheat oven to 400°. Heat pecans in a nonstick skillet over medium-low heat, stirring often, 4 minutes or until toasted and fragrant.

2. Microwave bacon at HIGH 2 to 3 minutes or until almost cooked but still pliable. Drain on paper towels. Cut bacon slices in half.

3. Process blue cheese and cream cheese in a blender or food processor until smooth. Stir in pecans. Spoon mixture into a zip-top plastic freezer bag (do not seal). Snip 1 corner of bag to make a small hole.

4. Cut a lengthwise slit down center of each date, cutting to but not through other side. Pipe cheese mixture into each date (about ½ tsp. each), and wrap each with 1 bacon slice. Secure each with a wooden pick. Arrange 1 inch apart on a lightly greased baking sheet.

5. Bake at 400° for 15 minutes or until bacon is crisp. Serve warm.

Make-Ahead Note: Prepare recipe as directed through Step 3. Cover and chill until ready to bake (up to 24 hours). Proceed as directed.

Smoked Salmon and Dill Pinwheels with Citrus Crème

Makes: 48 appetizer servings • Hands-On Time: 30 min. • Total Time: 2 hr., 30 min.

These delicate herbed mini crêpe rollups filled with lemon chive-infused crème fraîche and smoked salmon make an elegant appetizer during the holidays. Crêpes can be made ahead and frozen for up to one month.

- ⅔ cup milk
- ⅔ cup all-purpose flour
- 1 Tbsp. chopped fresh dill
- 2 tsp. butter, melted
- ¼ tsp. salt
- 2 large eggs
- ¾ cup crème fraîche or sour cream
- 1 Tbsp. chopped fresh chives
- 1 tsp. lemon zest
- ⅛ tsp. freshly ground pepper
- Wax paper
- 8 oz. thinly sliced smoked salmon

1. Process first 6 ingredients in a blender or food processor until smooth, stopping to scrape bowl as needed. Cover and chill 1 hour.

2. Stir together crème fraîche and next 3 ingredients in a small bowl. Cover and chill until ready to serve.

3. Place a lightly greased 10-inch nonstick skillet over medium heat until hot.

4. Pour ¼ cup batter into skillet; quickly tilt in all directions so that batter covers bottom of skillet with a thin film.

5. Cook about 1 minute. Carefully lift edge of crêpe with a spatula to test for doneness. The crêpe is ready to turn when it can be shaken loose from skillet. Turn crêpe over, and cook about 30 to 40 seconds or until done. Repeat procedure with remaining batter. Stack crêpes between sheets of wax paper until ready to fill.

6. Spread 1 side of each crêpe with 1½ Tbsp. crème fraîche mixture, leaving a ¼-inch border. Place 2 pieces of smoked salmon on each crêpe; roll up. Cut each rollup into 6 pieces. Secure with wooden picks. Cover and chill 1 to 4 hours.

Greek Meatballs with Tzatziki Sauce

Makes: 50 appetizer servings • Hands-On Time: 25 min. • Total Time: 50 min., including sauce

Use any leftovers for a tasty sandwich.

    1 lb. ground round
    1 lb. ground lamb
 2¼ cups soft, fresh breadcrumbs
    1 cup finely chopped onion
    4 garlic cloves, minced
    2 large eggs
    2 Tbsp. chopped fresh oregano
    2 Tbsp. chopped fresh mint
    2 Tbsp. harissa paste
   ½ tsp. salt
   ½ tsp. freshly ground pepper
       Tzatziki Sauce

1. Preheat oven to 425°. Combine first 11 ingredients in a large bowl, using hands. Shape mixture into 50 (1½-inch) meatballs. Place meatballs on a broiler rack in a roasting pan. Bake 15 minutes or until done. Serve with Tzatziki Sauce.

Make-Ahead Note: Meatballs can be made ahead and frozen before baking. Thaw meatballs in refrigerator before baking.

Note: Harissa is available in powder form and as a paste.

Tzatziki Sauce

Makes: 3 cups • Hands-On Time: 10 min. • Total Time: 10 min.

    2 cups Greek yogurt
    1 large English cucumber, peeled and chopped (about 2 cups)
    3 garlic cloves, minced
    1 Tbsp. chopped fresh dill
    2 Tbsp. extra virgin olive oil
    2 Tbsp. lemon juice
   ½ tsp. salt
   ½ tsp. freshly ground pepper

1. Combine all ingredients in a medium bowl. Cover and chill until ready to serve.

Note: Tzatziki sauce holds fine refrigerated up to 3 days.

Sweet and Savory Goat Cheesecakes with Quince Glaze

Makes: 24 servings • Hands-On Time: 35 min. • Total Time: 9 hr., 45 min.

These delightful miniature cheesecakes combine almond crackers and black pepper for a savory crust, a blend of goat and cream cheeses for the filling, and are then finished off with winter's best sweet quince preserves. Wine pairing suggestions would include Champagne, sparkling white wine, Roussanne or Sauvignon Blanc.

CRUST
  48 miniature paper baking cups
    1 (8.5-oz.) package almond crackers, crushed (2¼ cups)
   ½ tsp. freshly ground pepper
    6 Tbsp. butter, melted

FILLING
    1 (10.5-oz.) package goat cheese, softened
    6 oz. cream cheese, softened
   ¼ cup sugar
    1 tsp. lemon zest
    2 large eggs

GLAZE
    1 cup quince preserves

1. Prepare Crust: Preheat oven to 325°. Line 4 (12-cup) miniature muffin pans with miniature paper baking cups. Stir together almond cracker crumbs and black pepper. Stir in butter. Press crumb mixture into bottom of cups.
2. Bake at 325° for 5 minutes or until set. Cool on a wire rack. Reduce oven temperature to 275°.
3. Prepare Filling: Beat first 3 ingredients at medium speed with an electric mixer until blended and smooth. Add lemon zest, beating at low speed until well blended. Add eggs, 1 at a time, beating just until yellow disappears after each addition. Spoon 1 Tbsp. batter into each prepared crust.
4. Bake at 275° for 30 minutes or until center is almost set. Cool completely on wire rack (about 40 minutes). Cover and chill 8 hours.
5. Prepare Glaze: Heat quince preserves in a small saucepan over medium-low heat, stirring constantly, until melted and smooth. Remove from heat; cool 10 minutes. Top each cheesecake with 1 tsp. glaze.

Note: We tested with Keebler® Wheatables® Nut Crisps Roasted Almond crackers.

Dressy or Not
MAIN DISHES

WHETHER YOU'RE LOOKING FOR THE PERFECT DISH FOR THAT SPECIAL HOLIDAY MEAL, OR IN THE MOOD FOR A DELICIOUS WEEKNIGHT DINNER, THESE MAIN ATTRACTIONS ARE SURE TO IMPRESS.

QUICK & EASY
Glazed Pork Chops

Makes: 4 servings • Hands-On Time: 5 min. • Total Time: 28 min.

- 4 bone-in center-cut pork chops (1 inch thick)
- ¾ tsp. salt
- ½ tsp. freshly ground pepper
- 1 Tbsp. canola oil
- 1 Tbsp. butter
- ¾ cup apricot preserves
- 2 Tbsp. apple cider vinegar
- 2 tsp. fresh thyme leaves
- 1 tsp. grated fresh ginger
- 1 tsp. minced garlic
- Garnish: fresh thyme sprigs

1. Sprinkle pork with salt and pepper. Heat oil and butter in a large skillet over medium-high heat until butter melts. Add pork; cook 3 minutes on each side or until browned. Remove pork from skillet, reserving drippings in skillet; keep pork warm. Add preserves and next 4 ingredients, stirring to loosen particles from bottom of skillet. Cook over medium heat 4 minutes.
2. Return pork to skillet. Cook, uncovered, 13 minutes or just until a meat thermometer inserted in thickest portion registers 145°. Transfer pork to a serving platter; cover and let stand 3 minutes. Serve pork with sauce. Garnish, if desired.

Apricot-Ginger Glazed Pork Loin Roast

(pictured on facing page)
Makes: 6 servings • Hands-On Time: 29 min. • Total Time: 1 hr., 14 min.

Your guests will love this flavorful, tender roast with a hint of ginger and red pepper.

- 2 Tbsp. fresh thyme leaves
- 1 (4-lb.) boneless pork loin roast, trimmed
- 1 Tbsp. brown sugar
- ½ tsp. salt
- ½ tsp. garlic powder
- ⅛ tsp. ground red pepper
- Kitchen string
- 2 tsp. olive oil
- 2 tsp. grated fresh ginger
- 2 garlic cloves, minced
- 1 (12-oz.) jar apricot preserves
- 2 Tbsp. apple cider vinegar
- 1 Tbsp. light corn syrup
- Garnish: fresh thyme sprigs

1. Preheat oven to 375°. Sprinkle 2 Tbsp. thyme over pork, pressing gently to adhere. Combine brown sugar and next 3 ingredients. Rub pork with brown sugar mixture. Tie pork with kitchen string, securing at 1-inch intervals; place in a greased aluminum foil-lined roasting pan. Bake at 375° for 30 minutes.
2. Meanwhile, heat oil in a medium skillet over medium heat; add ginger and garlic. Sauté 1 minute or just until garlic is tender, but not browned. Stir in preserves, vinegar, and corn syrup. Bring to a boil; boil 1 minute. Divide glaze in half. Reserve half of glaze as a basting sauce. Set aside remaining half of glaze to serve with pork.
3. Remove pork from oven; brush ¼ cup basting glaze over roast. Bake 10 more minutes or until a meat thermometer inserted into thickest portion of pork registers 145°, brushing occasionally with basting glaze. Discard any remaining basting glaze. Remove pork from oven; let stand 3 minutes.
4. Transfer pork to a serving platter; remove string, and cut pork into slices. Serve with reserved glaze. Garnish, if desired.

Skillet-Seared Herb Rib Eyes

Makes: 6 servings • Hands-On Time: 25 min. • Total Time: 5 hr., 16 min.

Marinate these steaks overnight in the refrigerator for the fullest flavor.

- 6 (10- to 12-oz.) boneless rib-eye steaks (1¼ inches thick)
- ¼ cup olive oil
- 3 Tbsp. coarse-grained mustard
- 1 Tbsp. chopped fresh rosemary
- 1 Tbsp. chopped fresh oregano
- 1 Tbsp. chopped fresh thyme
- 1 Tbsp. coarsely ground pepper
- 2 tsp. coarse sea salt, divided

1. Place steaks in a large shallow baking dish. Combine oil and next 5 ingredients; drizzle over steaks, turning to coat. Cover and refrigerate at least 4 hours, turning occasionally.
2. Let steaks stand at room temperature 30 minutes.
3. Heat a cast-iron skillet over medium-high heat 3 minutes or until very hot. Sprinkle ½ tsp. sea salt over bottom of skillet. Place 3 steaks in skillet; cook 4 minutes. Remove steaks from skillet; sprinkle ½ tsp. salt in bottom of skillet. Return steaks to skillet, browned side up; cook 4 more minutes or until desired degree of doneness. Remove from skillet; cover and keep warm. Repeat procedure with remaining salt and steaks. Let steaks stand 5 minutes before serving.

Garlic-Herb Rib Roast

Makes: 6 to 8 servings • Hands-On Time: 20 min. • Total Time: 6 hr., 13 min.

For the best roast, ask the butcher for Prime grade and have the meat cut from the small or loin end.

- 1 (6½-lb.) 4-rib prime rib roast
- 10 garlic cloves, sliced
- 1½ Tbsp. coarsely ground pepper
- 1 Tbsp. coarse sea salt
- 2 Tbsp. olive oil, divided
- 3 Tbsp. coarse-grained mustard
- 2 Tbsp. chopped fresh rosemary
- 2 Tbsp. chopped fresh oregano
- 2 Tbsp. chopped fresh thyme

Garnishes: fresh rosemary, fresh oregano, and Lady apples

1. Let roast stand at room temperature 30 minutes. Cut ½-inch-deep slits in roast at 2-inch intervals. Stuff garlic slices into slits. Sprinkle pepper and salt over roast.

2. Preheat oven to 200°. Heat 1 Tbsp. oil in a 12-inch skillet over high heat. Cook roast in hot oil 4 minutes on each side or until browned. Place roast, fat side up, on a rack in a roasting pan. Spread mustard over top of roast; sprinkle with rosemary, oregano, and thyme. Drizzle with remaining 1 Tbsp. oil.

3. Bake at 200° for 5 hours or until a meat thermometer inserted in center registers 130° (rare). Let stand 15 minutes. Garnish, if desired.

Chicken Breasts Stuffed with Gouda and Prosciutto

Makes: 4 servings • Hands-On Time: 12 min. • Total Time: 47 min.

Bone-in chicken breasts help to keep the meat juicy and tender.

    2   oz. thinly sliced prosciutto
    3   Tbsp. butter, divided
 1¼   cups baby portobello mushrooms, finely chopped
    ¼   cup chopped shallot (1 large)
    1   tsp. chopped fresh thyme
    1   tsp. salt, divided
    ½   tsp. freshly ground pepper, divided
 1½   cups shredded Gouda cheese
    4   bone-in chicken breasts

1. Preheat oven to 500°. Cook prosciutto in a large nonstick skillet over medium-high heat 5 minutes or until crisp; remove prosciutto, reserving drippings in skillet, and drain on paper towels. Crumble prosciutto. Melt 2 Tbsp. butter in skillet. Add mushrooms, shallot, thyme, ½ tsp. salt, and ¼ tsp. pepper to drippings in pan; cook 5 minutes or until mushrooms are lightly browned and tender, stirring occasionally. Stir in cheese and prosciutto. Remove from heat.
2. Cut a slit (about 2 inches deep and 3 inches long; do not cut in half) in thick side of each chicken breast to form a pocket. Spoon one-fourth of mushroom mixture into each pocket. Pinch edges to seal; secure with wooden picks.
3. Place chicken in a 13- x 9-inch pan lined with aluminum foil. Melt remaining 1 Tbsp. butter; brush over chicken. Sprinkle chicken with remaining ½ tsp. salt and ¼ tsp. pepper. Bake at 500° for 25 minutes or until golden brown and done.

Chicken-Gouda Tetrazzini

Makes: 8 servings • Hands-On Time: 32 min. • Total Time: 1 hr., 20 min.

Use leftover cooked chicken or store-bought rotisserie chicken to speed up the prep of this classic dish.

  12   oz. uncooked vermicelli
    ½   cup butter
    ½   cup all-purpose flour
    4   cups milk
    ½   cup dry white wine
    1   tsp. chopped fresh thyme
    ½   tsp. salt
    ½   tsp. freshly ground pepper
    8   oz. Gouda cheese, shredded and divided
    4   cups chopped cooked chicken
    1   (8-oz.) package baby portobello mushrooms, sliced
    2   oz. thin prosciutto slices, cooked and crumbled

1. Preheat oven to 350°. Cook pasta according to package directions. Drain.
2. Meanwhile, melt butter in a Dutch oven over low heat; whisk in flour until smooth. Cook 1 minute, whisking constantly. Gradually whisk in milk and wine; cook over medium heat, whisking constantly, 12 minutes or until mixture is thickened and bubbly. Whisk in thyme, salt, pepper, and 1 cup cheese.
3. Remove pan from heat; stir in chicken, mushrooms, and pasta. Spoon mixture into a lightly greased 13- x 9-inch baking dish; sprinkle with remaining cheese. Bake at 350° for 35 minutes or until bubbly. Sprinkle with prosciutto.

Chicken-Gouda Tetrazzini

Marinated Grilled Quail with Candied Kumquats

Makes: 6 servings • Hands-On Time: 55 min. • Total Time: 9 hr., 30 min.

These delicate little birds are soaked in an Asian-inspired marinade, grilled to perfection, and served with Candied Kumquats. To complete the meal, we recommend serving the quail atop a bed of long-grain and wild rice with a side of sautéed haricots verts.

QUAIL
- 12 (3.5-oz.) semiboneless quail
- ¼ cup canola oil
- ¼ cup rice vinegar
- 3 Tbsp. soy sauce
- 2 Tbsp. honey
- 1 Tbsp. dark sesame oil
- 2 tsp. grated fresh ginger
- ½ tsp. dried crushed red pepper
- 3 garlic cloves, minced

CANDIED KUMQUATS
- 1¼ cups sugar
- 40 kumquats, quartered and seeded (about ¾ lb.)

1. Prepare Quail: Rinse quail, and pat dry. Combine canola oil and next 7 ingredients in a large zip-top plastic freezer bag; add quail. Seal bag, turning to coat. Chill at least 8 hours, turning once.

2. Meanwhile, prepare Candied Kumquats: Bring sugar and 1 cup water to a boil in a medium saucepan over medium-high heat. Boil 4 to 5 minutes or until sugar dissolves and mixture is clear, stirring occasionally.

3. Add kumquats; return to a boil. Reduce heat, and simmer, uncovered, 18 to 20 minutes or until kumquats are tender and mixture begins to thicken, stirring occasionally. Let cool completely. Cover and store in refrigerator up to 1 week.

4. Preheat grill to 350° to 400° (medium-high) heat. Remove quail from marinade, discarding marinade.

5. Grill quail, covered with grill lid, 5 to 6 minutes on each side or until done. Remove from grill, and let stand 5 minutes before serving.

6. Meanwhile, place kumquats in a small saucepan over low heat. Cook 3 to 4 minutes or until thoroughly heated, stirring occasionally. Arrange roasted quail on a serving platter. Spoon Candied Kumquats over quail.

Bacon-Wrapped Quail with Creamy Grits and Wild Mushroom Ragoût

Makes: 6 servings • Hands-On Time: 1 hr., 28 min. • Total Time: 2 hr., 53 min.

Served over creamy Southern grits with a white truffle oil-infused wild mushroom ragoût, this dish is nothing short of decadent.

QUAIL
- 12 (3.5-oz.) semiboneless quail
- 2 Tbsp. olive oil
- 2 Tbsp. chopped fresh sage
- 1 tsp. kosher salt
- ¼ tsp. freshly ground black pepper

CREAMY GRITS
- 2 cups chicken broth
- 2 cups milk
- ¼ tsp. kosher salt
- 1 cup uncooked stone-ground grits
- ¼ cup butter
- ¼ tsp. freshly ground pepper
- 2 oz. Parmigiano-Reggiano cheese, grated

MUSHROOM RAGOÛT
- 1 Tbsp. olive oil
- 1 Tbsp. butter
- 1 garlic clove, minced
- 2 (4-oz.) packages assorted fresh wild mushrooms
- ¼ tsp. kosher salt
- ⅛ tsp. freshly ground pepper
- 1½ tsp. white truffle oil

REMAINING INGREDIENTS
- 12 slices bacon
- 2 Tbsp. olive oil
- 1 Tbsp. all-purpose flour
- 1½ cups chicken broth
- 3 Tbsp. dry white wine
- 1 Tbsp. whipping cream

1. Prepare Quail: Rinse quail; pat dry. Combine 2 Tbsp. olive oil, sage, 1 tsp. kosher salt, and ¼ tsp. pepper in a small bowl. Rub mixture over quail. Place quail in a large zip-top plastic freezer bag. Chill at least 1 hour.

2. Meanwhile, prepare Creamy Grits: Bring 2 cups chicken broth and next 2 ingredients to a boil in a large heavy saucepan over medium-high heat. Gradually whisk in grits. Reduce heat to low; cover and simmer for 20 to 25 minutes or until thickened, stirring frequently. Remove from heat; stir in butter and pepper. Gradually stir in cheese. Cover and keep warm.

3. Prepare Mushroom Ragoût: Heat 1 Tbsp. olive oil and 1 Tbsp. butter in a large nonstick skillet over medium-high heat until butter melts. Add garlic; sauté 1 minute. Add mushrooms; cook 8 to 10 minutes or until golden, stirring occasionally. Remove from heat. Sprinkle with ¼ tsp. salt and ⅛ tsp. pepper; drizzle with truffle oil, and toss gently. Cover and keep warm.

4. Preheat oven to 375°. Remove quail from bag, discarding liquid. Wrap 1 bacon slice around each quail; secure with wooden picks.

5. Heat 1 Tbsp. olive oil in a large skillet over medium-high heat. Cook quail in hot oil 3 minutes on each side or until golden brown. Place 6 quail, breast side up, in a large shallow roasting pan. Repeat procedure with remaining 1 Tbsp. olive oil and place 6 quail, reserving 2 Tbsp. drippings in skillet.

Remove wooden picks from quail. Bake, uncovered, at 375° for 20 minutes or until done. Remove from pan; let stand 5 minutes.

6. Whisk flour into drippings in skillet until smooth. Add 1 cup broth and wine, whisking to loosen particles from bottom of skillet. Cook, whisking constantly, 5 minutes or until thickened. Whisk in cream. Remove from heat; cover and keep warm.

7. Microwave remaining ½ cup broth in a 1-cup glass measuring cup 30 seconds or until hot. Stir into grits until desired consistency. Spoon grits onto plates. Place 2 quail per serving on grits. Top with Mushroom Ragoût, and drizzle with sauce. Serve immediately.

Make-Ahead Note: You may chill quail up to 12 hours before preparing the grits.

Coriander-Crusted Salmon with Citrus Salsa

Makes: 8 servings • Hands-On Time: 27 min. • Total Time: 50 min.

For a pretty presentation, purchase a whole side of salmon.

    4   large navel oranges (2¾ lb.)
   2¼   tsp. kosher salt, divided
    ¼   cup chopped fresh cilantro
    ⅓   cup thinly sliced red onion
    1   tsp. lime zest
    ¼   cup fresh lime juice
    1   Tbsp. extra virgin olive oil
    ⅓   cup finely chopped seeded jalapeño peppers (about 3 large)
    1   (3 lb.) skinned salmon fillet
Parchment paper
    2   Tbsp. ground coriander
    1   tsp. freshly ground pepper

1. Preheat oven to 450°. Using a sharp, thin-bladed knife, cut a ¼-inch-thick slice from each end of oranges. Place one flat end down on a cutting board, and remove peel in strips, cutting from top to bottom following the curvature of fruit. Remove any remaining bitter white pith. Holding peeled orange in the palm of your hand, slice between membranes, and gently remove whole segments.

2. Combine orange segments, ¼ tsp. salt, cilantro, and next 5 ingredients in a medium bowl, tossing to combine.

3. Place salmon on a parchment paper-lined jelly-roll pan. Combine coriander, pepper, and remaining 2 tsp. salt in a small bowl; rub over fish. Bake at 450° for 23 to 25 minutes or until fish flakes with a fork. Transfer salmon to a rimmed platter; top with citrus salsa.

Salmon Tacos with Jalapeño-Citrus Slaw

Makes: 8 servings • Hands-On Time: 20 min. • Total Time: 30 min.

The coriander dry rub forms an amber-colored crust that's both tasty and impressive.

- 1 large navel orange
- 3 cups angel hair slaw
- ⅓ cup chopped red onion
- ¼ cup chopped fresh cilantro
- ¼ cup finely chopped seeded jalapeño peppers (about 2 small)
- 1 tsp. lime zest
- 2 Tbsp. fresh lime juice
- 3 Tbsp. extra virgin olive oil, divided
- 1¾ tsp. kosher salt, divided
- 2 Tbsp. ground coriander
- 1 tsp. freshly ground black pepper
- 1 (2-lb.) skinned salmon fillet, cut into 4 pieces
- 16 (6-inch) corn or flour tortillas

1. Using a sharp, thin-bladed knife, cut a ¼-inch-thick slice from each end of orange. Place one flat end down on a cutting board, and remove peel in strips, cutting from top to bottom following the curvature of fruit. Remove any remaining bitter white pith. Holding peeled orange in the palm of your hand, slice between membranes, and gently remove whole segments. Chop orange segments, and place in a large bowl. Add slaw and next 3 ingredients.

2. Stir together lime zest, lime juice, 2 Tbsp. oil, and ¼ tsp. salt in a small bowl; pour over slaw mixture, tossing gently to combine.

3. Combine remaining 1½ tsp. salt, coriander, and pepper; rub over fish. Heat remaining 1 Tbsp. oil in a large skillet over medium-high heat. Add salmon; cook 2 to 3 minutes on each side or until fish flakes with a fork. Remove fish from skillet; flake fish with a fork.

4. Spoon slaw into tortillas; top with salmon. Serve immediately.

Super
SIMPLE SIDES

ACCENTUATE YOUR HOLIDAY TABLE
WITH THESE EASY SIDES REQUIRING
ONLY 5 INGREDIENTS EACH.

Sour Cream and Chive Potato Bake

Makes: 12 servings • Hands-On Time: 18 min. • Total Time: 1 hr., 13 min.

Sour cream gives whipped potatoes new life in this super-easy side dish.

- 5   lb. baking potatoes, peeled and cut into 1-inch pieces
- 1   Tbsp. kosher salt, divided
- ¼   cup butter, cut into pieces
- 1   (16-oz.) container sour cream
- ¼   cup chopped fresh chives
- 2   Tbsp. butter, melted
- Garnish: chopped fresh chives

1. Preheat oven to 400°. Butter a 13- x 9-inch baking dish.
2. Bring potatoes, 2 tsp. salt, and water to cover to a boil in a large Dutch oven; cook 25 to 30 minutes or until tender. Drain well.
3. Beat potatoes, ¼ cup butter, and remaining 1 tsp. salt at medium speed with a heavy-duty electric stand mixer until smooth. Stir in sour cream and ¼ cup chives. Spoon mixture into prepared dish. Drizzle with melted butter.
4. Bake at 400° for 30 minutes or until top is lightly browned. Garnish, if desired.

MAKE AHEAD
Bacon-Caramelized Onion-Spinach Bake

Makes: 8 to 10 servings • Hands-On Time: 20 min. • Total Time: 1 hr., 5 min.

This creamed spinach is decadent and rich—perfect for a special occasion. For best results, use good quality smoked bacon.

- 1   lb. bacon
- 2   large sweet onions, coarsely chopped
- 4   (10-oz.) packages frozen chopped spinach, thawed
- 1   (8-oz.) package cream cheese, softened
- 1   cup half-and-half
- ½   tsp. salt
- ¼   tsp. freshly ground pepper

1. Preheat oven to 350°. Lightly grease an 11- x 7-inch baking dish.
2. Cook bacon, in batches, in a large skillet over medium heat 8 to 10 minutes or until crisp; remove bacon, reserving drippings in skillet. Crumble bacon.
3. Sauté onions in hot drippings 20 minutes or until onions are deep golden brown. Remove from heat.

4. Drain spinach well, pressing between paper towels. Combine cream cheese, next 3 ingredients, spinach, half of bacon, and onions. Spoon mixture into prepared dish. Sprinkle with remaining bacon. Bake at 350° for 25 minutes or until bubbly and lightly browned.

Make Ahead: Assemble the casserole in advance, and refrigerate it overnight. Let stand at room temperature 30 minutes before baking.

Italian-Style Baked Beans

Makes: 8 servings • Hands-On Time: 20 min. • Total Time: 45 min.

Salty pancetta jazzes up this simple bean dish that comes together in a snap.

- ½   cup chopped pancetta (about 3 oz.)
- 1   sweet onion, finely chopped (2 cups)
- 3   (15-oz.) cans cannellini beans, drained
- 2   (14½-oz.) cans diced tomatoes with basil, garlic, and oregano
- 1½ cups coarsely crushed Italian-flavored crostini

1. Preheat oven to 400°. Sauté pancetta and onion in a Dutch oven coated with cooking spray over medium heat 5 minutes or until translucent.
2. Add beans and tomatoes. Bring to a boil; reduce heat, and simmer, uncovered, 8 minutes or until thoroughly heated.
3. Spoon bean mixture into a greased 11- x 7-inch baking dish; sprinkle with crumbs.
4. Bake, uncovered, at 400° for 25 minutes or until bubbly and lightly browned. Let stand 5 minutes before serving.

PANCETTA VS. PROSCIUTTO

These Italian meats pack a punch of flavor, but what's the difference between the two? Pancetta is very similar to bacon except that it's not cut into thin strips. Cured in salt and spices, it's best served cooked. Prosciutto, however, is dry-cured ham and is similar to country ham. It can be served cooked or not.

Honey-Roasted Beets and
Asparagus

Honey-Roasted Beets and Asparagus

Makes: 6 servings • Hands-On Time: 10 min. • Total Time: 40 min.

If your beets are on the large side, cut them into thin wedges
so they'll cook quickly to fork-tender doneness.

 1   lb. fresh asparagus
1½ lb. fresh beets
 2   Tbsp. olive oil
 ½   tsp. salt
 ½   tsp. freshly ground pepper
 1   cup chopped walnuts
 3   Tbsp. honey
 2   oz. crumbled feta cheese

1. Preheat oven to 450°. Snap off and discard tough ends of
asparagus. Cut asparagus in half crosswise. Trim beet stems
to 1 inch. Peel beets, and cut into wedges. Place beets in a
single layer on a 15- x 10-inch jelly-roll pan or roasting pan.
Drizzle with olive oil; sprinkle with salt and pepper. Toss to
coat.
2. Roast at 450° for 20 minutes or until beets are almost
tender. Add asparagus and walnuts to pan; toss to coat. Roast
10 to 12 more minutes or until asparagus and beets are tender.
Drizzle with honey. Sprinkle with cheese just before serving.

Pearled Couscous with Mushrooms, Chestnuts, and Pecorino

Makes: 4 servings • Hands-On Time: 4 min. • Total Time: 16 min.

These oversized pearls of pasta are larger than traditional
couscous and have a heartier texture.

 1   (4.7-oz.) package roasted garlic and olive oil pearled
     couscous
 ¼   cup butter
 1   (8-oz.) package presliced baby portobello mushrooms
 ¼   tsp. freshly ground pepper
 ½   cup chopped chestnuts, toasted
 ½   tsp. chopped fresh thyme (optional)
 ½   cup (2 oz.) shredded pecorino Romano cheese

1. Prepare couscous according to package directions.
2. Melt butter in a medium skillet over medium-high heat. Add
mushrooms and pepper; sauté 8 minutes or until tender. Stir
in couscous, chestnuts, and if desired, thyme. Sprinkle with
cheese.

Fruited Basmati Rice Pilaf

Makes: 4 to 6 servings • Hands-On Time: 10 min. • Total Time: 36 min.

Almonds add star power to this simple dish.

  2 garlic cloves, minced
  2 Tbsp. olive oil
  2 cups chicken broth
  1 cup basmati rice
  1 cup chopped dried mixed fruit
  ½ tsp. salt
  ½ tsp. freshly ground pepper
  ½ cup sliced almonds
  Garnish: chopped green onions

1. Sauté garlic in hot oil in a medium saucepan over medium heat 1 minute or until tender. Add broth, next 4 ingredients, and ½ cup water. Bring to a boil. Cover, reduce heat to low, and cook 20 minutes or until rice is tender.
2. Meanwhile, preheat oven to 350°. Bake almonds in a single layer in a shallow pan 6 to 8 minutes or until lightly toasted and fragrant.
3. Fluff rice mixture with a fork. Stir in almonds. Garnish, if desired.

Horseradish-Spiked Cauliflower Gratin

Makes: 8 servings • Hands-On Time: 45 min. • Total Time: 1 hr., 45 min.

A horseradish béchamel makes this dish creamy and rich.

  2 small heads cauliflower (about 2½ lb.), separated into florets
  ¼ cup butter
  ¼ cup all-purpose flour
  3 cups milk
  6 Tbsp. refrigerated horseradish
  1 tsp. salt
  ½ tsp. freshly ground pepper

1. Preheat oven to 375°. Cook cauliflower in boiling salted water to cover 5 minutes or until crisp-tender; drain.
2. Melt butter in a heavy saucepan over low heat; whisk in flour until smooth. Cook 1 minute, whisking constantly. Gradually whisk in milk; cook over medium heat, whisking constantly, until mixture is thickened and bubbly. Remove from heat; stir in horseradish and next 2 ingredients.
3. Pour one-third of sauce into a lightly greased 3-qt. gratin dish or 13- x 9-inch baking dish. Add cauliflower; pour remaining sauce over cauliflower.
4. Bake at 375° for 1 hour or until golden brown.

Asiago-Breadcrumb Cauliflower Gratin: For an extra cheesy version with a crunchy topping, combine 1½ cups fresh French breadcrumbs, ½ cup grated Asiago cheese, and 5 Tbsp. melted butter in a medium bowl. Sprinkle breadcrumb topping over gratin in baking dish and bake as directed.

Citrus-Glazed Roasted Winter Vegetables

Makes: 8 servings • Hands-On Time: 25 min. • Total Time: 1 hr., 5 min.

The natural sweetness in winter root vegetables is coaxed forth by roasting them and further enhanced with a citrus-honey glaze.

- 2 lb. parsnips
- 2 lb. carrots
- 2 Tbsp. olive oil
- 1 tsp. salt
- ½ tsp. freshly ground pepper
- 1 tsp. orange zest
- ¼ cup fresh orange juice (about 1 orange)
- ¼ cup honey
- 1 tsp. fresh thyme leaves
- Garnish: fresh thyme sprig

1. Preheat oven to 450°. Peel first 2 ingredients, and diagonally slice into 1-inch pieces. Combine parsnips, carrots, oil, salt, and pepper in a large bowl. Toss to coat. Divide vegetables between 2 lightly greased 18- x 13-inch half-sheet pans or roasting pans.

2. Bake at 450° for 25 minutes. Stir once, and bake 15 to 20 more minutes or until vegetables are tender. Meanwhile, whisk together orange zest, juice and next 2 ingredients.

3. Drizzle honey mixture over roasted vegetables; toss gently. Garnish, if desired.

Maple-Ginger
Roasted Acorn Squash

Maple-Ginger Roasted Acorn Squash

Makes: 8 servings • Hands-On Time: 8 min. • Total Time: 1 hr., 18 min.

Maple syrup and peppery fresh ginger give this winter squash a flavor makeover.

  2 medium-size acorn squash (about 3 lb.)
  1 Tbsp. olive oil
  ½ tsp. kosher salt
  ⅔ cup firmly packed brown sugar
  ½ cup butter, softened
  ⅓ cup maple syrup
  1 tsp. grated fresh ginger

1. Preheat oven to 350°. Cut squash in half lengthwise, cutting through stem and bottom ends. Remove and discard seeds. Place 2 squash halves, cut sides down, in an 11- x 7-inch baking dish. Cover tightly with plastic wrap; fold back a small corner to allow steam to escape. Microwave at HIGH 5 minutes or until squash is barely tender. Repeat with remaining squash. Let cool completely. Cut squash into ½-inch wedges.
2. Place squash, cut sides up, in a large roasting pan. Drizzle with olive oil; sprinkle with salt.
3. Bake at 350° for 20 minutes. Meanwhile, combine brown sugar and next 3 ingredients in a small saucepan; cook over medium heat until butter is melted. Spoon mixture over squash. Bake 40 more minutes or until tender, basting with glaze after 20 minutes. Arrange squash on a serving platter; drizzle with glaze.

QUICK & EASY
Seared Radicchio with Balsamic Glaze

Makes: 10 servings • Hands-On Time: 23 min. • Total Time: 23 min.

Simple seared radicchio is a quick, colorful, and delicious side dish. A leaf chicory, this vegetable is ubiquitous in Italian cuisine. Searing or grilling mellows its bitter and spicy bite. The key to perfectly seared radicchio is making sure the pan is extremely hot; the final result should be slightly charred radicchio wedges.

  5 heads radicchio (about 2½ lb.), quartered
  3 Tbsp. olive oil
  ½ tsp. kosher salt
  ½ tsp. freshly ground pepper
  ¼ cup balsamic glaze
  ⅔ cup grated fresh Parmigiano-Reggiano cheese
  2 Tbsp. chopped fresh flat-leaf parsley

1. Heat a large grill pan over medium-high heat until very hot. Brush radicchio wedges with olive oil, and sprinkle with salt and pepper. Place radicchio, 1 cut side down, on grill pan. Cook, in batches, 3 to 4 minutes, turning to brown on all sides. Transfer to a serving platter.
2. Drizzle balsamic glaze over radicchio. Sprinkle with cheese and parsley.

Six Sweet
REASONS

SEARCHING FOR A DESSERT TO WOW EVERYONE THIS HOLIDAY? LOOK NO FURTHER WITH THESE OVER-THE-TOP SWEET ENDINGS.

Raspberry Italian Meringue Layer Cake

Makes: 16 servings • Hands-On Time: 41 min. • Total Time: 3 hr., 40 min., including filling and frosting

The St. Honoré piping tip adds a festive and elegant flourish to this stately cake but the cake can just as easily be frosted by hand.

1¼ cups butter, softened
2¼ cups sugar
3¾ cups cake flour
  2 Tbsp. baking powder
  1 tsp. salt
  9 egg whites
1½ cups milk
  1 Tbsp. vanilla extract
  ½ tsp. almond extract
Raspberry Filling
Italian Meringue Frosting

1. Preheat oven to 350°. Beat butter and sugar at medium speed with a heavy-duty electric stand mixer until creamy, beating about 5 minutes or until well blended.
2. Sift together cake flour and next 2 ingredients. In another bowl, whisk together egg whites and next 3 ingredients. Gradually add dry ingredients to butter mixture alternately with milk mixture, beginning and ending with dry ingredients. Beat at low speed just until blended after each addition.
3. Spoon batter into 3 greased and floured 9-inch round cake pans. Bake at 350° for 25 to 30 minutes or until a wooden pick inserted in center comes out clean. Cool in pans on wire racks 10 minutes; remove from pans to wire racks, and cool completely (about 1 hour).
4. Split cake layers. Spread about ⅓ cup Raspberry Filling between each cake layer. Spread Italian Meringue Frosting on sides of cake. Insert St. Honoré metal tip into a large decorating bag; fill with remaining frosting. Pipe in a decorative pattern on top of cake.
5. If desired, brown meringue frosting using a kitchen torch, holding torch 1 to 2 inches from cake and moving torch back and forth.

Raspberry Filling

Makes: 2 cups • Hands-On Time: 37 min. • Total Time: 1 hr., 7 min.

4½ cups fresh raspberries
  1 cup sugar
  2 tsp. lemon juice
  ¼ cup cornstarch
  1 Tbsp. black raspberry liqueur

1. Combine raspberries, sugar, and lemon juice in a medium saucepan. Bring to a boil over medium-high heat. Cook 15 minutes or until fruit is very soft, stirring often. Remove from heat; press raspberry mixture through a wire-mesh strainer using the back of a spoon to squeeze out juice. Discard pulp and seeds. Let cool. Whisk together cornstarch and ½ cup strained raspberry mixture in a saucepan until smooth. Stir in remaining strained raspberry mixture.
2. Bring to a boil over medium heat, whisking constantly. Boil, whisking constantly, 1 minute or until thickened. Remove pan from heat.
3. Place pan in ice water; whisk occasionally until cool. Stir in liqueur. Cover and chill 30 minutes.

Note: We tested with Chambord liqueur.

Italian Meringue Frosting

Makes: 5 cups • Hands-On Time: 16 min. • Total Time: 16 min.

1¼ cups sugar
  4 egg whites
  ¼ tsp. cream of tartar

1. Stir together sugar and ½ cup water in a small heavy saucepan over medium heat, and cook, without stirring, until a candy thermometer registers 240° (soft ball stage), about 10 minutes.
2. Beat egg whites at medium speed with a heavy-duty electric stand mixer until foamy; add cream of tartar, beating until soft peaks form. Slowly add hot syrup mixture, beating constantly. Beat until stiff peaks form and frosting is desired consistency.

Make-Ahead Note: For best results, make the Raspberry Filling as your first step in preparing this cake. You want it to be chilled when the time comes to assemble the cake.

Blood Orange Crêpe Gâteau

Makes: 12 to 16 servings • Hands-On Time: 2 hr. • Total Time: 3 hr.

Many layers filled with sweet blood orange curd make this cake grand and elegant.

CANDIED BLOOD ORANGES
1 cup sugar
2 medium blood oranges, cut into ⅜-inch slices
Wax paper

BLOOD ORANGE CURD
1 cup sugar
¼ cup butter
4 tsp. blood orange zest
⅔ cup fresh blood orange juice
½ cup grenadine
6 large eggs, beaten

CRÊPE GÂTEAU
2½ cups milk
2 cups all-purpose flour
⅔ cup superfine sugar
¼ tsp. salt
6 large eggs, slightly beaten
1 cup butter, melted and divided
2½ tsp. vanilla extract, divided
1 cup heavy cream
2 Tbsp. powdered sugar
¼ cup pomegranate seeds

1. Prepare Candied Blood Oranges: Bring sugar and 1 cup water to a boil in a 6-qt. Dutch oven. Place orange slices, in a single layer, on top of sugar mixture; reduce heat and simmer, uncovered, 30 minutes. Turn orange slices over, and simmer 30 more minutes or until pulp is translucent and rinds are softened.

2. Using a slotted spoon, transfer slices to a wax paper–lined plate. Let cool completely; cover and chill.

3. Meanwhile, prepare Blood Orange Curd: Combine first 5 ingredients in a 4-qt. heavy saucepan. Cook over medium heat, whisking constantly, 3 minutes or until butter melts and sugar dissolves. Gradually whisk about one-fourth of hot mixture into beaten eggs in a thin stream; add egg mixture to hot mixture, whisking constantly. Cook over low heat 12 minutes, whisking constantly, until thickened. Remove from heat. Place heavy-duty plastic wrap directly on warm custard (to prevent a film from forming); chill thoroughly (mixture will thicken as it cools).

4. Meanwhile, prepare Crêpe Gâteau batter: Whisk together first 5 ingredients, 6 Tbsp. melted butter, and 2 tsp. vanilla in a large bowl. Cover and chill 1 hour.

5. Heat a crêpe pan or 8-inch nonstick skillet over medium heat. Remove pan from heat. Brush pan with melted butter. Pour 2 Tbsp. batter into skillet; quickly tilt in all directions so that batter covers bottom of skillet with a thin film.

6. Cook about 1 minute. Carefully lift edge of crêpe with a spatula to test for doneness. (The crêpe is ready to turn when it can be shaken loose from skillet.) Turn crêpe over, and cook about 30 to 40 seconds or until done. Repeat procedure with remaining batter, brushing pan with remaining melted butter as necessary to prevent sticking. Let cool completely.

7. To serve, place 1 crêpe on a cake plate or stand. Spread crêpe with about 2 Tbsp. curd, and top with another crêpe. Repeat with remaining crêpes and curd.

8. Beat cream and remaining ½ tsp. vanilla until foamy; gradually add powdered sugar, beating until soft peaks form. Mound whipped cream mixture in center of crêpe stack. Top with Candied Blood Oranges, and sprinkle with pomegranate seeds. Serve immediately.

Make Ahead: Batter may be made ahead and chilled up to 1 day.

Baklava Cheesecake

Makes: 10 servings • Hands-On Time: 18 min. • Total Time: 11 hr., 50 min.

Purchase prepared baklava from a local Greek restaurant, or, if you have time, make your own. It's the hidden surprise in each slice of this decadent dessert.

1½ cups walnut halves
1 cup sugar, divided
2 Tbsp. unsalted butter, melted
2½ (8-oz.) packages cream cheese, softened
1 (8-oz.) package mascarpone cheese, softened
3 large eggs
1 tsp. almond extract
¼ tsp. salt
5 (3-oz.) pieces baklava
12 walnut halves
Honey Syrup

1. Preheat oven to 350°. Pulse 1½ cups walnuts and ¼ cup sugar in a food processor 4 or 5 times or until walnuts are finely ground. Add butter; pulse until mixture resembles coarse sand. Press mixture firmly on bottom of a lightly greased 9-inch springform pan. Bake at 350° for 12 to 14 minutes or until lightly browned. Cool on a wire rack.
2. Reduce oven temperature to 300°. Beat cream cheese, mascarpone, and remaining ¾ cup sugar at medium speed with an electric mixer until blended. Add eggs, 1 at a time, beating just until blended after each addition. Add almond extract and salt, beating at low speed just until blended.
3. Cut each baklava piece into 2 small triangles, about 2 x 3 inches. Arrange baklava pieces in a ring over baked crust, with pointy end of each piece pointing towards center and wide ends around outside edge of pan. Pour batter over baklava into baked crust.
4. Bake at 300° for 1 hour and 20 minutes or until edges are set and center is almost set. Remove cheesecake from oven; gently run a knife around edge of cheesecake to loosen. Cool completely on a wire rack (about 2 hours). Cover and chill 8 hours. Remove sides of pan. Top with walnut halves. Serve with Honey Syrup.

Honey Syrup

Makes: ½ cup • Hands-On Time: 2 min. • Total Time: 3 min.

½ cup honey
2 tsp. orange blossom water
½ tsp. orange zest

1. Combine all ingredients in a small saucepan. Bring to a boil over medium-high heat. Remove from heat; cool completely.

Note: Find orange blossom water at upscale food markets or cook stores.

4. Bake at 325° for 30 minutes or until a wooden pick inserted in center comes out almost clean. Cool in pans on wire racks 5 minutes; remove from pans to wire racks, and cool completely (about 20 minutes).

5. Spread ½ cup Ganache, about 1 cup Honey-Glazed Pecans, and ½ cup Caramel Sauce between layers, spreading Ganache to edges and letting it drip down sides. Spread ½ cup Ganache over top of torte. Top with remaining 1 cup Honey-Glazed Pecans; drizzle with 3 Tbsp. Caramel Sauce.

Ganache

Makes: 1⅔ cups • Hands-On Time: 2 min. • Total Time: 2 min.

    1 (12-oz.) package semisweet chocolate morsels
    ⅔ cup whipping cream

1. Microwave chocolate morsels and whipping cream in a large microwave-safe bowl at HIGH 1 minute or until melted and smooth, stirring after 30 seconds.

Honey-Glazed Pecans

Makes: about 3 cups • Hands-On Time: 10 min. • Total Time: 30 min.

    1 Tbsp. butter
    3 Tbsp. honey
    2½ cups pecan halves
       Parchment paper

1. Melt butter in a large nonstick pan over medium heat; add honey, stirring until blended. Add pecans, stirring constantly until coated. Cook 6 to 8 minutes, stirring often, or until almost all liquid is absorbed and pecans are toasted.

2. Working quickly, pour glazed pecans onto parchment paper-lined baking sheet, separating pecans in a single layer. Let cool completely (about 20 minutes).

Caramel Sauce

Makes: 1⅔ cups • Hands-On Time: 1 min. • Total Time: 3 min.

    1 (13.4-oz.) can dulce de leche
    ⅓ cup whipping cream

1. Microwave dulce de leche and whipping cream in a 2-cup glass measuring cup or microwave-safe bowl at HIGH 1 minute, stirring at 30-second intervals.

FIX IT FASTER: Use packaged brownie mix for the layers, melt tub fudge frosting, and top with purchased sugared pecans.

EDITOR'S FAVORITE   MAKE AHEAD
Turtle Brownie Torte

Makes: 10 servings • Hands-On Time: 37 min. • Total Time: 1 hr., 29 min. (including ganache, pecans, and caramel sauce)

Serve any extra Caramel Sauce or Ganache over ice cream.

      Wax paper
      Unsweetened cocoa
    2 (4-oz.) bittersweet chocolate baking bars, chopped
    1¼ cups butter, cut into pieces
    2 cups sugar
    4 large eggs
    1½ cups all-purpose flour
    ¼ tsp. baking powder
    ¼ tsp. salt
    1 Tbsp. vanilla extract
       Ganache
       Honey-Glazed Pecans
       Caramel Sauce

1. Preheat oven to 325°. Grease 3 (8-inch) round cake pans; line with wax paper. Grease wax paper; lightly dust pans with cocoa.

2. Microwave chocolate and butter in a large microwave-safe bowl at MEDIUM (50% power) 1 to 1½ minutes or until melted and smooth, stirring at 30-second intervals. Let cool 5 minutes. Add sugar, stirring until blended. Add eggs, 1 at a time, whisking just until blended after each addition.

3. Combine flour, baking powder, and salt. Gradually add to chocolate mixture, whisking just until blended. Stir in vanilla. Spread batter evenly into prepared pans.

Brown Sugar-Ginger Cookie Trifle

Makes: 12 servings • Hands-On Time: 29 min. • Total Time: 3 hr., 3 min.

The cookie spread used in this trifle is what makes it special.

COOKIES
    1   cup butter, softened
    1   cup sugar
    1   large egg
    1   tsp. vanilla extract
2½   cups all-purpose flour
    ½   tsp. salt
    ¾   cup chopped crystallized ginger

PUDDING
    ⅓   cup sugar
    2   Tbsp. cornstarch
    2   Tbsp. unsweetened cocoa
    ¼   tsp. salt
    3   cups milk
    2   egg yolks
    1   (14-oz.) jar Belgian caramelized cookie spread, divided

REMAINING INGREDIENT
    4   cups sweetened whipped cream

1. Prepare Cookies: Beat butter at medium speed with an electric mixer until creamy; gradually add sugar, beating until fluffy. Add egg and vanilla; beat well. Combine flour and salt; add to butter mixture, beating just until blended. Stir in ginger. Shape dough into 2 (6-inch) logs. Wrap logs in wax paper; chill 2 hours or until firm. Preheat oven to 350°. Cut dough into ¼-inch-thick slices. Place on ungreased baking sheets. Bake at 350° for 12 minutes or until almost golden. Remove to wire racks, and let cool completely. Break cookies into pieces.

2. Prepare Pudding: Whisk together first 4 ingredients in a heavy saucepan. Gradually whisk in milk and egg yolks. Bring to a boil over medium heat, whisking constantly. Boil, whisking constantly, 1 minute or until thickened. Remove pan from heat. Whisk in 1 cup cookie spread. Place pan in ice water; whisk pudding occasionally until cool. Place plastic wrap directly onto pudding (to prevent a film from forming); chill 1 hour.

3. Place 3½ cups cookie pieces in bottom of a 4-qt. trifle bowl. Spoon half of pudding over cookies; top with half of whipped cream. Repeat layers with 3½ cups cookies, remaining pudding, and remaining whipped cream. Sprinkle remaining cookies over top of trifle. Microwave remaining spread in a microwave-safe bowl at HIGH 30 seconds or until melted. Drizzle spread over trifle.

Note: We tested with Biscoff spread.

Gingersnap-Meyer Lemon Meringue Tart

(pictured on page 92)
Makes: 10 to 12 servings • Hands-On Time: 25 min. • Total Time: 3 hr., 55 min.

If Meyer lemons are unavailable, substitute equal amounts of regular lemon juice and orange juice.

GINGERSNAP CRUST
    2   cups crushed gingersnaps (about 40 gingersnaps)
    5   Tbsp. butter, melted

FRESH MEYER LEMON CURD
1½   cups sugar
    ¼   cup cornstarch
    3   large eggs
    3   egg yolks
    ⅔   cup fresh Meyer lemon juice
1½   Tbsp. Meyer lemon zest
    ½   cup cold butter, cut into pieces

ITALIAN MERINGUE
    1   cup sugar
    2   Tbsp. light corn syrup
    3   egg whites
    Garnish: Meyer lemon slices

1. Prepare Gingersnap Crust: Preheat oven to 350°. Stir together gingersnap crumbs and butter. Firmly press mixture on bottom and up sides of a 10-inch tart pan. Bake at 350° for 9 minutes or until golden and fragrant. Cool in pan on a wire rack 30 minutes.

2. Meanwhile, prepare Fresh Meyer Lemon Curd: Whisk together 1½ cups sugar and cornstarch in a heavy saucepan. Whisk in eggs and egg yolks. Stir in lemon juice. Bring to a boil over medium heat, whisking constantly. Boil, whisking constantly, 1 to 1½ minutes or until thickened. Remove pan from heat. Stir in lemon zest and butter.

3. Fill a large bowl with ice. Place pan containing lemon curd in ice, and let stand, stirring occasionally, 15 minutes. Spread lemon curd over prepared crust. Place heavy-duty plastic wrap directly on lemon curd (to prevent a film from forming); chill 2 hours. (Mixture will thicken as it cools.)

4. Prepare Italian Meringue: Preheat broiler with oven rack 8 inches from heat. Combine ¼ cup water, sugar, and corn syrup in a small heavy saucepan; cook over medium heat, stirring constantly, until clear. Cook, without stirring, until a candy thermometer registers 240° (soft ball stage). Beat egg whites at high speed with an electric mixer until soft peaks form; slowly add syrup mixture, beating constantly. Beat until stiff peaks form. Spoon meringue in center of tart; spread to within 2 inches of edge of tart. Broil 3 to 4 minutes or until golden brown. Cool completely on a wire rack. Chill 1 hour. Garnish, if desired.

Share

Share the joys of the season with loved ones, and create one-of-a-kind gifts from your kitchen.

Make to
DECORATE

USE ON-HAND KITCHEN INGREDIENTS TO
CREATE GORGEOUS CHRISTMAS BAUBLES
TO GIVE AS GIFTS OR SPRUCE
UP YOUR HOME.

Salt Dough Gift Tags

Makes: about 2 dozen • Hands-On Time: 1 hr., 55 min. • Total Time: 4 hr., 25 min.

Salt dough is a simple, versatile dough perfect for making Christmas gift tags and ornaments. Use coffee instead of water for a gingerbread-colored dough, or knead in paste food coloring.

DOUGH
2½ cups all-purpose flour, divided
1 cup salt
Paste food coloring (optional)

REMAINING MATERIALS
Drinking straw
Parchment paper
Decoupage glue*
Coarse glitter
Tray to catch glitter
Ribbon

1. Preheat oven to 250°. Combine 2 cups flour and salt in bowl of a heavy-duty stand mixer. Add 1 cup water to bowl, and beat at medium speed until blended.

2. Turn dough out onto a lightly floured surface. Knead 10 minutes or until dough is smooth and elastic, adding ½ cup remaining flour as necessary to prevent sticking. Knead food coloring into dough, if desired. Roll out half of dough to ¼-inch thickness. (Keep remaining half of dough covered to prevent drying.) Cut dough with desired cookie cutters. Use a straw to create a hole at the top of each shape for threading ribbon. Place tags on parchment paper-lined baking sheets. Repeat with remaining dough.

3. Bake at 250° for 2 hours or until tags are dry. Cool on pans 10 minutes; remove from pans to wire racks to cool completely.

4. Paint tags completely on front with decoupage glue. Set on tray, and sprinkle with glitter until completely covered, shaking off excess. Let dry completely. Thread ribbon through holes in tops of tags.

*We tested with Mod Podge.

Variation: Paint tags with acrylic paint, and use them as ornaments for the Christmas tree. Coat finished ornaments with shellac to preserve for years.

STOCK YOUR MAKE-TO-DECORATE KITCHEN

When the weather turns colder, everyone snuggles in to the warmth of a cozy home. Take advantage of this special time and make merry crafts to share with family and friends on chilly autumn and winter evenings. Be sure to have these craft items on hand to make the Christmas decorations featured in this chapter:

Decoupage glue
Craft glue
Glitter
Paste food coloring
Cookie cutters of all shapes and sizes
Christmas ribbons
Acrylic paints
Spray paint
Paint pens
Hot glue gun

Twine
Paint brushes
Foam wreath
Wooden skewers
Rubber aspirator
Drinking straws

More ideas for giving:
• Use a copier to make copies of vintage Christmas designs from past Christmas cards; cut out. Glue cutouts onto inexpensive photo frames. Once dry, paint with decoupage glue to seal.
• Place fresh cranberries and rosemary sprigs in the bottom of a clear vase. Fill with water and fresh flowers.
• Roll pinecones in peanut butter and birdseed. Tie with a ribbon and hang outside for your feathered friends.

{1}

Spice-Scented Ornaments

Makes: 32 (2¼-inch) ornaments • Hands-On Time: 40 min. • Total Time: 3 hr., 10 min.

Use these cutouts as Christmas ornaments, gift tags, place markers, or string them across a kitchen window. Their fragrance will fill the air.

- ¾ cup applesauce
- ½ cup ground cinnamon
- ½ cup ground cardamom
- Drinking straws
- Ribbon (optional)
- Black, gold, or silver paint pens (optional)

1. Preheat oven to 200°. Stir together first 3 ingredients in a small bowl until a smooth ball forms. Working with one-fourth of dough at a time, roll dough to ¼-inch thickness between 2 sheets of heavy-duty plastic wrap. Peel off top sheet of plastic wrap.

2. Cut dough into desired shapes with 2¼-inch cookie cutters. Make a hole at top of ornament using a straw. Place ornaments on an ungreased baking sheet.

3. Bake at 200° for 2 hours and 30 minutes. Transfer ornaments to wire racks to cool completely.

4. If desired, insert ribbon through holes, and tie ends of ribbon.

* *

{1} These ornaments make the sweetest drink markers. Be sure to use miniature cookie cutters in enough shapes for the number of guests you'll be entertaining. {2} Personalize your place settings with fragrant Christmas trees. {3} These scented ornaments with festive holiday greetings are the perfect addition to your tree.

* *

{2}

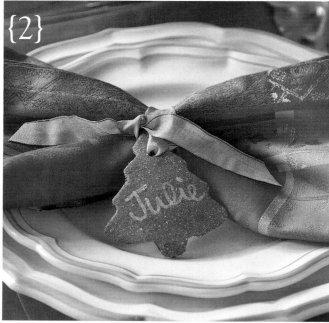

{3}

Candy Garland

Brighten up your mantel this year with a vibrant (and edible) garland. We used rod candies, but experiment with your favorite shapes and colors.

  2 lb. multicolored rod candies
Hot glue gun
Multicolored ribbons

1. Measure length of mantel. Double the mantel length to determine the length of the garland.
2. Glue candy wrapper ends together using a hot glue gun. Let cool.
3. Gather garland every 12 inches, and tie multiple ribbons together to create a bow. Repeat for entire length of garland.

{4} Make your mantel merry with vibrantly colored vases and a playful candy garland. Gather fresh greenery clippings of Fraser fir and snowberries to tuck into the vases. Fill clear canisters with any leftover candy for Santa to satisfy his sweet tooth after barrelling down the chimney.

Sugar Cookie Trees

Makes: 15 trees • Hands-On Time: 40 min. • Total Time: 3 hr., 45 min.

Kids will love to help you decorate these festive trees!

1½	cups butter, softened
2	cups granulated sugar
4	large eggs
1	tsp. vanilla extract
5	cups all-purpose flour
2	tsp. baking powder
½	tsp. salt
1½	tsp. green gel food coloring
1	(4⅓-oz.) tube green decorating icing
	Small yellow star sprinkles
	Sanding sugar

1. Beat butter at medium speed with an electric mixer until creamy. Gradually add granulated sugar, beating well. Add eggs and vanilla, beating well.
2. Combine flour, baking powder, and salt; gradually add to butter mixture, beating at low speed just until blended. Beat in food coloring. Cover and chill dough 2 hours or until firm.
3. Preheat oven to 375°. Roll out dough to ¼-inch thickness on a lightly floured surface. Cut with a 3-inch or 5-inch cutter into tree shapes. Place cookies 1 inch apart onto ungreased baking sheets.
4. Bake at 375° for 10 to 12 minutes or until set, but not browned. Cool on baking sheets 2 minutes. While cookies are warm, cut half of cookies in half vertically. Transfer to wire racks, and cool completely.
5. Use icing to glue 2 matching cookie halves at right angles on opposite sides of the center of each whole cookie. Decorate cookies using additional icing to attach sprinkles and sanding sugar.

* *

{1} Cut dough into varying sizes of Christmas tree shapes for a festive tree village. {2} Be sure to cut cookies in half while they're still warm or else they'll crumble. {3} Carefully glue tree halves onto whole Christmas trees and hold into place with icing. Use a flat surface for standing the trees upright. A container of fluffy fake snow or flaked coconut works well as a wintry-looking base for the trees..

* *

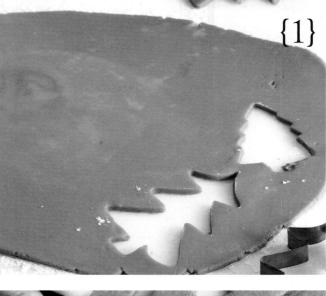

Dried Citrus Ornaments

Makes: 45 ornaments • Hands-On Time: 27 min. • Total Time: 12 hr., 57 min.

Showcase the bounty of citrus season with these sparkling gems.

- 2 grapefruit, cut into ⅛-inch slices
- 2 oranges, cut into ⅛-inch slices
- 2 lemons, cut into ⅛-inch slices
- 2 limes, cut into ⅛-inch slices
- ½ cup decoupage glue*
- ¾ cup coarse glitter
- Twine

1. Preheat oven to 200°. Place grapefruit and orange slices in a single layer on a large cooling rack on a large baking sheet. Place lemon and lime slices on a cooling rack on a separate baking sheet.

2. Bake fruit slices at 200° for 2 hours; turn slices over. Bake 30 more minutes; remove lemon and lime slices from oven. Let cool completely on rack.

3. Bake orange and grapefruit slices 1 more hour; remove orange slices from oven. Let cool completely on rack. Bake grapefruit slices 1 more hour; remove grapefruit slices from oven. Let cool completely on rack.

4. Brush edges of dried fruit slices with decoupage glue. Roll edges in glitter. Return to racks on baking sheets to dry completely (8 hours or overnight).

5. Cut a small hole near the edges of fruit slices. Thread desired lengths of twine through holes. Tie ends of twine together to create hangers.

*We tested with Mod Podge.

Spice Candles

Illuminate the room with a festive glow and the sweet scent of cinnamon.

2 small (3-inch) white pillar candles
30 small cinnamon sticks
2 large (5-inch) white pillar candles
30 large cinnamon sticks
Hot glue gun
Twine

1. For small candle, glue small cinnamon sticks around base of candle using hot glue gun. Let cool, and tie with twine.
2. For large candle, glue large cinnamon sticks around base of candle using hot glue gun. Let cool, and tie with twine.

Tangerine Pomander Balls

Try using other citrus fruits like oranges, grapefruit, lemons, and limes.

    8 tangerines
    Whole cloves
    Whole star anise (optional)
    Hot glue gun
    3 Tbsp. ground ginger
    3 Tbsp. ground cinnamon
    1 Tbsp. ground allspice
    Ribbon

1. Pierce tangerine rind with a fork, wooden pick, or ice pick in desired decorative design. Place cloves in holes, rosette sides out. Decorate with whole star anise using a glue gun, if desired.

2. Combine ginger, cinnamon, and allspice. Roll tangerines in spice mixture, and shake off excess. Tie with decorative ribbon and store in a dry place.

* *

{1} Pierce the skin of the tangerine using a wooden pick or wooden skewer in desired decorative pattern. {2} Place cloves, rosette sides out, into pierced holes. Glue whole star anise into a decorative pattern using hot glue gun, if desired. Roll tangerines in spice mixture and shake off excess. {3} Wrap holiday ribbon around the tangerine, being careful to avoid the clove designs. Tie securely into bows. As pomander balls dry, the warm scents of citrus and spice will permeate your room.

* *

Peppermint Wreath

For a different twist, try green striped spearmints or red and green swirled peppermints.

Red spray paint
1   (12-inch) foam wreath
4   lb. assorted peppermint candies, unwrapped
Hot glue gun
Thick red, green or white ribbon

1. Spray paint the foam wreath; let dry.
2. Attach peppermint candies in rows (not overlapping) to foam wreath using hot glue gun. Allow glue to dry before attaching ribbon to the top of the wreath.

{1} Kids and grown-ups alike will love to make this whimsical holiday wreath. Leave the hot glue step to the adults and let little hands help with the unwrapping of the candies. Try smaller foam wreaths, available at crafts stores, for another option. {2} This sweet wreath is a fun way to welcome guests. Store the wreath indoors, or brush with decoupage glue to seal and enjoy outdoors.

{1}

{2}

Mini Gingerbread House Place Card Holder

Makes: 30 mini houses • Hands-On Time: 1 hr., 15 min. • Total Time: 4 hr., 45 min.

GINGERBREAD CUTOUTS

- ¾ cup unsalted butter, softened
- 1½ cups dark brown sugar
- 2 large eggs
- 1 cup dark molasses
- 6 cups all-purpose flour
- 1 tsp. baking soda
- 4 tsp. ground ginger
- 4 tsp. ground cinnamon
- ½ tsp. baking powder
- ¾ tsp. ground allspice
- ½ tsp. salt
- Parchment paper

ICING

- 8 cups powdered sugar
- 6 Tbsp. meringue powder
- 6 Tbsp. warm water
- 1 (8-oz.) container white sparkling sugar
- Assorted snowflake sprinkles
- Crushed peppermint candies
- 15 miniature chocolate caramel cookie bars, cut diagonally in half*

1. Prepare cutouts: Beat butter at medium speed with an electric mixer until creamy; gradually add brown sugar, beating well. Add eggs, molasses, and 1 Tbsp. water; beat well.

2. Combine flour and next 6 ingredients; stir well. Gradually add to butter mixture, beating at low speed until blended. Shape dough into 3 balls. Cover and chill 2 hours.

3. Preheat oven to 350°. Working with 1 portion of dough at a time, roll to ⅛-inch thickness on a lightly floured surface. Using templates (on page 171), cut out 10 fronts, 10 backs, 20 walls, and 20 roof pieces, removing excess dough with the tip of a knife and re-rolling excess dough as necessary.

4. Place cutouts on a large baking sheet lined with parchment paper. Bake at 350° for 10 to 12 minutes or until golden. Transfer parchment paper with cookies to a wire rack to cool completely. Repeat procedure with remaining dough, cutting parts for 10 houses from each portion of dough.

5. Prepare icing: Beat powdered sugar, meringue powder, and 6 Tbsp. warm water at high speed with a heavy-duty stand mixer, using whisk attachment, until stiff and glossy peaks form. Place a damp cloth directly on surface of icing (to prevent a crust from forming) while assembling houses.

6. Pipe a line of icing along edge of each short side of 1 wall piece. Press wall piece between 1 front piece and 1 back piece, holding in place until all 3 pieces adhere. Pipe a line of icing along edge of each short side of another wall piece, and position it between front piece and back piece to complete 4 walls of 1 house, holding in place to adhere.

7. Working on 1 side of the house at a time, pipe icing around the perimeter of 1 roof piece. Attach roof piece to house. Repeat with another roof piece, piping icing at peak of roof to adhere. Repeat procedure with remaining cutouts and enough icing for assembly. Let houses stand 1 hour or until dry.

8. Pipe icing on roof and on corners of houses in a decorative pattern. Decorate as desired, using remaining icing to attach sprinkles and candies to houses. Cut a ⅛-inch slit in flat end of each cookie bar half. Attach diagonal end of cookie bar half to roof to form a chimney, using icing to adhere. Pipe outlines for doors and windows with icing. Let stand until completely dry. Insert place cards into slits in chimneys.

*We tested with Twix bars.

{1} Gather your favorite Christmas sprinkles and holiday candies to decorate these tiny houses. Kids will love to join in on the fun. {2} Carefully pipe frosting as the glue to hold the sides and roof of the gingerbread houses. {3} Gently press the side and roof pieces onto the frosting. Hold in place for a few minutes to allow the frosting to dry before moving on. Decorate as desired with sprinkles, candies, and additional frosting.

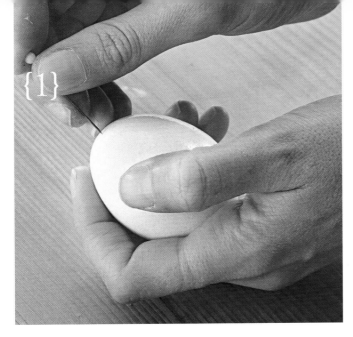

Ukranian Christmas Eggs

Blown eggs aren't just for Easter. Make and decorate these beautiful treasures to set in a bowl, egg cups, or tie with ribbons to hang on the tree.

 1 dozen eggs, at room temperature
Straight pin
Wooden skewer
Rubber aspirator
 1 cup vinegar
Acrylic paints
Red and green food coloring
White paint pens (ultra-fine, fine, or medium point)

1. Wash and dry eggs with dish soap. Gently poke a hole at each end of the egg with a straight pin. Twist the straight pin until the hole is about 2 millimeters.
2. Insert the wooden skewer through 1 end, and "scramble" the egg inside. Place the rubber aspirator over 1 hole, and blow the contents into a bowl. Repeat with remaining eggs.
3. Combine vinegar and 1 cup water. Submerge eggs in vinegar mixture, and clean thoroughly; let dry.
4. Paint eggs with acrylic paints or dye eggs according to food coloring package directions for dyeing eggs, let dry, and decorate with paint pens.

* *

{1} Using a straight pin, poke a hole in each end of the egg. Use a skewer to pierce and scramble the egg yolk inside the egg. {2} Hold the egg over a bowl, and blow out the contents using a rubber aspirator. Wash the hollow eggs with a vinegar solution. Dry completely before decorating. {3} Use acrylic paints to decorate eggs or dye eggs with food coloring and decorate with paint pens.

* *

Pickled & PRESERVED

GIVE A JAR OF JOY THIS HOLIDAY SEASON WITH
THESE CANNED FAVORITES.

Satsuma Marmalade with Star Anise

Makes: 5 (½-pt. jars) • Hands-On Time: 19 min. • Total Time: 53 min.

A winter delicacy, satsuma oranges are prized for having an easy-to-peel skin and practically no seeds.

- 3 large satsuma oranges (about 2 lb.)
- 1 lemon
- 2 Tbsp. minced fresh ginger
- ⅛ tsp. baking soda
- 5 star anise
- 1 (1.75-oz.) package powdered pectin
- 4 cups sugar

1. Scrub fruit. Rinse well, and pat dry. Carefully remove rind from fruit using a vegetable peeler, making sure to avoid white pith; coarsely chop rind to measure 1 cup.
2. Place rind, ginger, next 2 ingredients, and 2½ cups water in a Dutch oven. Bring to a boil over high heat; cover, reduce heat, and simmer 20 minutes, stirring occasionally.
3. Meanwhile, remove and discard white pith from fruit; cut fruit into ½-inch-thick slices. Remove seeds, and coarsely chop fruit to measure 2 cups fruit and juices.
4. Add fruit and juices to cooked rind. Bring to a boil; reduce heat and simmer, uncovered, 10 minutes. Stir in pectin. Bring to a rolling boil that cannot be stirred down; stir in sugar. Return to a rolling boil; boil 1 minute. Remove from heat; skim off any foam. Ladle marmalade and 1 star anise into each of 5 hot, sterilized jars, filling to within ¼-inch from top. Seal jars. Cool completely. Store in refrigerator 1 week or until set before serving. Store up to 3 weeks in refrigerator.

Green Tomato Chutney

Makes: 4 (½-pt.) jars • Hands-On Time: 31 min. • Total Time: 2 hr., 16 min.

This chutney can be made as chunky as you like it.

- 1½ cups cider vinegar
- 1¼ cups firmly packed light brown sugar
- 1 cup chopped onion
- ½ cup golden raisins
- ½ cup currants
- ¼ cup honey
- 2 tsp. mustard seeds
- 2 tsp. kosher salt
- 4 green tomatoes (1¾ lb.), finely chopped
- 2 garlic cloves, chopped
- 2 canned chipotle peppers in adobo sauce, chopped
- 1 (2-inch) piece fresh ginger, chopped

1. Combine all ingredients in a Dutch oven. Bring to a boil; reduce heat, and simmer 1½ hours or until thickened, stirring occasionally.
2. Spoon chutney into hot jars, filling to ½ inch from top. Remove air bubbles; wipe jar rim. Cover at once with metal lids, and screw on bands. Process in boiling water bath 15 minutes; cool.

Pickled Red Onions

Makes: 12 (1-pt.) jars • Hands-On Time: 1 hr., 30 min. • Total Time: 1 hr., 50 min.

Colorful spiced and pickled red onions make a beautiful holiday gift. Packed into pint jars, these sweet-and-sour beauties are delicious on sandwiches, in tossed green or creamy salads, served with cold or warm meats, or just eaten straight from the jar.

- 5 qt. white vinegar
- 9 cups sugar
- 3 Tbsp. pickling salt
- 3 Tbsp. whole allspice, divided
- 3 Tbsp. whole black peppercorns, divided
- 10 large red onions (10 lb.), cut into ⅓-inch slices
- 24 bay leaves
- 24 dried red chile peppers
- 2 tsp. whole cloves

1. Combine first 3 ingredients, 1 Tbsp. allspice, and 1 Tbsp. peppercorns in a large stockpot. Bring to a boil over medium-high heat. Separate onion slices into rings; add to vinegar mixture. Bring to a boil; reduce heat, and simmer 10 minutes.
2. Meanwhile, place 2 bay leaves and 2 chile peppers in each of 12 hot jars. Divide cloves, remaining allspice, and remaining peppercorns evenly among jars.
3. Using a slotted spoon, transfer onion to jars. Pour vinegar mixture into jars, filling to ½ inch from top. Remove air bubbles; wipe jar rims. Cover at once with metal lids, and screw on bands. Process in boiling water bath 10 minutes; cool.

THE POWER OF PECTIN

While many fruits naturally contain enough of this gelling agent, some recipes call to add a little more for an extra thickening boost. We tested with Sure-Jell powdered pectin.

Red or Green Pepper Jelly

Makes: 6 (½-pt. jars) • Hands-On Time: 38 min. • Total Time: 2 hr., 48 min.

Pepper jelly spooned over cream cheese and served with crackers is holiday comfort food. Make your own jelly with this easy recipe and then consider gift giving.

¾ cup coarsely chopped sweet onion
5 large jalapeño peppers, seeded and coarsely chopped (¾ cup)
2 large red or green bell peppers, seeded and cut into 1-inch pieces to equal 2 cups
1 cup cider vinegar
1 (1.75-oz.) package powdered fruit pectin
5 cups sugar
Red or green food coloring (optional)

1. Pulse first 3 ingredients in a food processor 5 or 6 times or until very finely chopped.

2. Combine pepper mixture, vinegar, and pectin in a large Dutch oven; bring to a rolling boil. Quickly stir in sugar. Return to a boil; boil 4 minutes, stirring constantly. Remove from heat, and skim off foam with a metal spoon. Add food coloring, if desired.

3. Pour hot jelly into hot jars, filling to ¼ inch from top; wipe jar rims. Cover at once with metal lids, and screw on bands.

4. Process in boiling water bath 10 minutes; cool.

Note: To serve, spoon ⅓ cup Red Pepper Jelly over half of 1 round of Brie or 1 (8-oz.) package cream cheese. Spoon ⅓ cup Green Pepper Jelly over remaining half of Brie or cream cheese.

Bread and Butter Pickled Vegetables

Makes: 5 (1-pt.) jars • Hands-On Time: 57 min. • Total Time: 1 hr., 10 min.

Perfect for snacking, gift giving, or as an appetizer, Bread and Butter Pickled Vegetables will be your go-to recipe for the busy holiday season because it will already be on your pantry shelf.

1 small head cauliflower, broken into small florets
1 cup pearl onions
1 medium-size red bell pepper, cut into 1-inch pieces
1 medium-size green bell pepper, cut into 1-inch pieces
1 cup haricots verts, halved crosswise
4 carrots, peeled and cut diagonally into 1-inch slices
3 cups white wine vinegar (5% acidity)
¾ cup sugar
1 Tbsp. kosher salt
1 tsp. mustard seeds
1 tsp. black peppercorns
8 garlic cloves, halved
3 small dried red chile peppers
1 cup drained whole pepperoncini salad peppers

1. Bring 4 quarts water to a boil in a Dutch oven. Add cauliflower and onions; cook 3 minutes. Remove vegetables with a slotted spoon; plunge into ice water to stop the cooking process; drain. Repeat procedure with bell pepper and haricot verts, cooking 1 minute. Repeat procedure with carrot, cooking 3 minutes. (Cooking carrot last prevents staining the other vegetables orange.)
2. Bring vinegar, next 6 ingredients, and 3 cups water to a boil in a large saucepan, stirring until sugar dissolves.
3. Pack vegetables and pepperoncini peppers in hot jars, filling to ½ inch from top. Pour hot vinegar mixture over vegetables, filling to ½ inch from top. Remove air bubbles; wipe jar rims. Cover at once with metal lids, and screw on bands. Process in boiling water bath 10 minutes; cool.

Ginger-Cardamom Pear Butter

Makes: 7 (½-pt. jars) • Hands-On Time: 1 hr., 38 min. • Total Time: 8 hr., 30 min.

There is nothing quite like homemade preserves, especially when made from fruit at its peak. Purchase fresh pears at your local farmers' market in autumn or even better, make it a fun family outing and "pick your own" at a local orchard. Save a bit by purchasing "seconds," those pears that might have minor blemishes or bruises, as they are perfectly fine to use for pear butter. This recipe calls for a quarter-bushel of sweet ripe pears.

12 lb. ripe Anjou, Bartlett or Comice pears, peeled and coarsely chopped
 2 cups sugar
 ¼ cup fresh lemon juice
 1 Tbsp. grated fresh ginger
1½ tsp. ground cardamom

1. Process pear, in batches, in a food processor or blender until smooth, stopping to scrape down sides as needed.
2. Stir together pear puree, sugar, and remaining ingredients in a large stockpot. Bring to a boil; reduce heat, and maintain at a light simmer for 7 hours or until very thick, stirring occasionally. (Pear mixture should cling to an inverted spoon.)
3. Spoon butter into hot jars, filling to ¼ inch from top; remove air bubbles, and wipe jar rims. Cover at once with metal lids, and screw on bands. Process in boiling water bath 10 minutes.

Canning 101

The process of "putting up" preserves and pickles takes advantage of a farmers' market bounty, is fun, and provides jars of gifts to give away at Christmastime. Follow these easy tips, and you'll be guaranteed success.

Equipment Needed:

Boiling Water Canner: This large, deep stockpot is ideal for heat processing canning jars and is equipped with a lid and a rack. The rack is designed with handles to be lifted up, allowing easy removal of the hot jars. A stockpot and round cake rack are acceptable substitutes; just note that the pot used must be large enough to completely surround and immerse the jars in water (ideally the pot will be 3 inches deeper than the height of the jars).

Canning Jars and Lids: Glass canning jars specifically designed for canning are available at most grocery and hardware stores. They have a unique threaded neck design intended for the lid and screw-on band to ensure closure. While screw-on bands may be used multiple times, the flat canning lids may be used only once due to the unique food-safe seal coating on the underside of each lid.

Jar Lifters: These coated tongs are uniquely shaped to lift hot jars out of the boiling water bath. Do not use metallic, uncoated tongs because they can scratch the jars.

Canning Funnels: These special funnels have wide openings and fit neatly inside the mouths of the jars, making them easier to fill.

Nonmetallic Spatulas: These help when removing air bubbles from the filled jars.

Step-By-Step:

1. Prepare the jars, lids, and bands.

Wash the jars, lids, and bands with hot, soapy water. Place the jars in the boiling water canner with water to cover; cover and bring to a simmer. Keep the jars hot until ready for use. Meanwhile, place the lids in a small saucepan with water to cover; simmer, but do not boil. Keep the lids hot until ready for use.

2. Prepare the recipe.

3. Fill the jars.

Work with one jar at a time (keep remaining jars in boiling water canner). Place the hot jar on a wooden surface or towel (heat-protected surface), and fill, using a canning funnel, if desired. Leave the proper amount of headspace as specified by the recipe. Remove any air bubbles with a nonmetallic spatula. Adjust the headspace if necessary. Wipe the jar rim with a clean damp cloth, and place the hot jar lid on top, sealing the contents of the jar. Place the screw-on bands on the jar and screw on the band until tight. Do not overtighten. Return jar to boiling water canner, and repeat with remaining jars and lids.

4. Process the filled jars.

Adjust the water level, if necessary, to cover the jars by at least one inch. Cover and bring water to a boil. Follow boiling instructions specified in the recipe.

5. Allow the jars to cool.

Remove the lid from the canner; let jars cool 5 minutes. Remove the jars from the hot water, and place upright on a towel in a draft-free area. Let cool, undisturbed, for 24 hours.

6. Check the seals.

Once the jars have cooled for 24 hours, remove the screw-on bands, and press down on the centers of the lids. If they are sealed properly, the lids will be concave and show no movement. However, if they "pop" or are easily pressed down, these unsealed jars must be reprocessed or refrigerated immediately.

Canning Considerations:

• Always select the best-quality ingredients for the recipe. If any produce is bruised, carefully remove the damaged spots before proceeding with the recipe.

• Be sure to use only new canning jars (as opposed to antiques) that can be fitted with current two-piece metal closures.

• Do not use any screw bands or lids that show signs of damage or rusting. Never reuse flat canning lids.

• To prevent breakage, make sure you pour hot food into hot jars, and avoid exposing hot jars to a surface with a great temperature difference.

• For best quality, use home-canned foods within one year.

Love It? GET IT!

Many items pictured in the book are one-of-a-kind or no longer available—we've listed similar looks when possible. Source information is current at the time of publication. If an item is not listed, its source is unknown.

• pages 10-11—**patterned flatware:** Sabre, en.sabre.fr; **burlap place mats:** Lamb's Ears, Ltd., Birmingham, AL, (205) 802-5700, www.lambsearsltd.com.

• pages 20-21—**flatware:** Sabre, en.sabre.fr.

• page 26—**glass:** Table Matters, Birmingham, AL, (205) 879-0125, www.table-matters.com.

• page 28—**napkin:** Bromberg's, Birmingham, AL, (205) 871-3276, www.brombergs.com.

• page 32—**slate board:** West Elm, (888) 922-4119, www.westelm.com.

• page 34—**silver basket:** Bromberg's, Birmingham, AL, (205) 871-3276, www.brombergs.com.

• page 35—**glass dome:** Henhouse Antiques, Birmingham, AL, (205) 918-0505, www.shophenhouseantiques.com.

• page 38—**platter:** Bromberg's, Birmingham, AL, (205) 871-3276, www.brombergs.com.

• page 39—**jam jar and silver basket:** Bromberg's, Birmingham, AL, (205) 871-3276, www.brombergs.com.

• pages 42-43—**napkin and place mats:** Pottery Barn, (888) 779-5176, www.potterybarn.com; **red plates:** Table Matters, Birmingham, AL, (205) 879-0125, www.table-matters.com. Fortunata, (404) 351-1096, www.fortunatainc.com.

• page 50—**decorations:** Flowerbuds,

Inc., Birmingham, AL, (205) 970-3223, www.flowerbudsinc.com.

• pages 52-53—**decorations:** Scot Wedgeworth.

• page 55—**decorations:** Scot Wedgeworth.

• page 61—**decorations:** Scot Wedgeworth.

• page 64—**decorations:** Scot Wedgeworth; The Oaks, Centreville, AL, (205) 225-0044.

• page 65—**decorations:** The Oaks, Centreville, AL, (205) 225-0044.

• pages 66-68—**decorations:** Scot Wedgeworth.

• page 69—**decorations:** The Oaks, Centreville, AL, (205) 225-0044.

• page 72—**decorations:** The Oaks, Centreville, AL, (205) 225-0044.

• page 73—**decorations:** Kristin McPhearson.

• page 79—**decorations:** Scot Wedgeworth.

• pages 84-85—**decorations:** Don Huff, Susan Huff, Beth Jordan; The Caroline House at Briarwood Presbyterian Church.

• page 94—**pie plate:** Williams-Sonoma, (877) 812-6235, www.williams-sonoma.com.

• page 97—**plate and rectangular baking dish:** Bromberg's, Birmingham, AL, (205) 871-3276, www.brombergs.com.

• page 112—**spoon:** At Home, Birmingham, AL, (205) 879-3510, www.athome-furnishings.com, Table

Matters, Birmingham, AL, (205) 879-0125, www.table-matters.com. Montes Doggett, (866) 834-9857, www.montesdoggett.com; **linen:** Studiopatro, (415) 775-3432, www.studiopatro.com.

• page 118—**plates:** Vietri, (919) 245-4180, www.vietri.com; **wine glasses:** Vietri, (919) 245-4180, www.vietri.com; **platter:** Dbo Home, (860) 364-6008, www.dbohome.com.

• page 120—**glass with colored band:** Tricia's Treasures, Birmingham, AL, (205) 871-9779, www.triciastreasures.us.

• page 132—**platter:** Vietri, (919) 245-4180, www.vietri.com.

• page 140—**plates:** Dbo Home, (860) 364-6008, www.dbohome.com; **linen:** Pehr, (647) 343-8024, www.pehrdesigns.com.

• page 143—**marble cake plate:** America Retold, (518) 822-0100, www.americaretold.com.

• page 148—**wrapping paper:** Anthropologie, (800) 309-2500, www.anthropologie.com.

• page 151—**vases:** Eigen Arts, www.eigenarts.com.

• page 156—**pedestal:** America Retold, (518) 822-0100, www.americaretold.com.

• page 166—**spreader:** Sabre, en.sabre.fr.

• page 168—**spoon:** Sabre en.sabre.fr; **tags:** Alice Goldsmith Ceramics, (718) 636-2248, www.alicegoldsmithceramics.com.

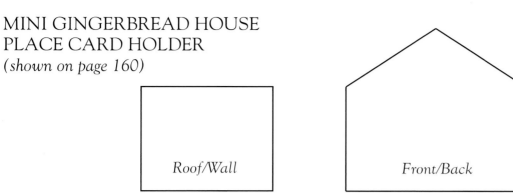

MINI GINGERBREAD HOUSE
PLACE CARD HOLDER
(shown on page 160)

Roof/Wall

Front/Back

Thanks to these CONTRIBUTORS

Thanks to the following businesses

A'Mano
Anthropologie
At Home
Bromberg's
Chickadee
Davis Wholesale Florist, Inc.
Flowerbuds, Inc.
Henhouse Antiques
Jojo Home
Lagniappe Designs Inc.
Lamb's Ears, Ltd.
Lisa Flake of Caldwell Flake Interiors
Marjorie Johnston & Company Interiors and Design
Mulberry Heights
The Oaks, Centreville, AL
Pottery Barn
Scot Wedgeworth of Scot Wedgeworth Weddings,
    Events, and Entertaining (star of the reality
    series *Bama Glama* on the Food Network)
Smith's Variety
Table Matters
Tricia's Treasures
West Elm
Williams-Sonoma

Thanks to the following homeowners

Arthur & Alison Bagby
Cindy Bankston
Rock & Emelita Braun
Brian & Lauren Burgess
Butch & Carol Cauthen
Baker & Alison Chambliss
Brennan & Alli Denning
James & Rita Dixon
Lisa Flake
Randy & Lisa Freeman
Don & Susan Huff
Kelli Kelly
Ken & Kristin McPhearson
Dr. Suzanne Oparil
Sandy & Meg Sullivan
Teresa Suttle
John & Laurie Wilbanks

GENERAL INDEX

METRIC EQUIVALENTS

The recipes that appear in this cookbook use the standard United States method for measuring liquid and dry or solid ingredients (teaspoons, tablespoons, and cups). The information in the following charts is provided to help cooks outside the U.S. successfully use these recipes. All equivalents are approximate.

Metric Equivalents for Different Types of Ingredients

A standard cup measure of a dry or solid ingredient will vary in weight depending on the type of ingredient. A standard cup of liquid is the same volume for any type of liquid. Use the following chart when converting standard cup measures to grams (weight) or milliliters (volume).

Standard Cup	Fine Powder (ex. flour)	Grain (ex. rice)	Granular (ex. sugar)	Liquid Solids (ex. butter)	Liquid (ex. milk)
1	140 g	150 g	190 g	200 g	240 ml
¾	105 g	113 g	143 g	150 g	180 ml
⅔	93 g	100 g	125 g	133 g	160 ml
½	70 g	75 g	95 g	100 g	120 ml
⅓	47 g	50 g	63 g	67 g	80 ml
¼	35 g	38 g	48 g	50 g	60 ml
⅛	18 g	19 g	24 g	25 g	30 ml

Useful Equivalents for Liquid Ingredients by Volume

¼ tsp					=		1 ml	
½ tsp					=		2 ml	
1 tsp					=		5 ml	
3 tsp	=	1 Tbsp			=	½ fl oz	=	15 ml
		2 Tbsp	=	⅛ cup	=	1 fl oz	=	30 ml
		4 Tbsp	=	¼ cup	=	2 fl oz	=	60 ml
		5⅓ Tbsp	=	⅓ cup	=	3 fl oz	=	80 ml
		8 Tbsp	=	½ cup	=	4 fl oz	=	120 ml
		10⅔ Tbsp	=	⅔ cup	=	5 fl oz	=	160 ml
		12 Tbsp	=	¾ cup	=	6 fl oz	=	180 ml
		16 Tbsp	=	1 cup	=	8 fl oz	=	240 ml
		1 pt	=	2 cups	=	16 fl oz	=	480 ml
		1 qt	=	4 cups	=	32 fl oz	=	960 ml
						33 fl oz	=	1000 ml = 1 l

Useful Equivalents for Dry Ingredients by Weight

(To convert ounces to grams, multiply the number of ounces by 30.)

1 oz	=	¹⁄₁₆ lb	=	30 g
4 oz	=	¼ lb	=	120 g
8 oz	=	½ lb	=	240 g
12 oz	=	¾ lb	=	360 g
16 oz	=	1 lb	=	480 g

Useful Equivalents for Length

(To convert inches to centimeters, multiply the number of inches by 2.5.)

1 in					=	2.5 cm		
6 in	=	½ ft			=	15 cm		
12 in	=	1 ft			=	30 cm		
36 in	=	3 ft	=	1 yd	=	90 cm		
40 in					=	100 cm	=	1 m

Useful Equivalents for Cooking/Oven Temperatures

	Fahrenheit	Celsius	Gas Mark
Freeze water	32° F	0° C	
Room temperature	68° F	20° C	
Boil water	212° F	100° C	
Bake	325° F	160° C	3
	350° F	180° C	4
	375° F	190° C	5
	400° F	200° C	6
	425° F	220° C	7
	450° F	230° C	8
Broil			Grill

RECIPE INDEX

Peppermint Wreath, page 158

Holiday PLANNER

GETTING READY FOR THE HOLIDAY SEASON IS HALF THE FUN! FROM DECORATING THE HOUSE TO ENTERTAINING GUESTS, THIS HELPFUL PLANNER MAKES ORGANIZING EASY. REFER TO IT WHEN YOU START MAKING PLANS FOR NEXT YEAR'S CHRISTMAS.

NOVEMBER *2012*

Sunday	Monday	Tuesday	Wednesday
4	5	6	7
11	12	13	14
18	19	20	21
25	26	27	28

Thursday	Friday	Saturday
1	*2*	*3*
8	*9*	*10*
15	*16*	*17*
Thanksgiving *22*	*23*	*24*
29	*30*	

Holiday-Ready Pantry

Be prepared for seasonal cooking and baking by stocking up on these items.

- ☐ Assorted coffees, teas, hot chocolate, and eggnog
- ☐ Wine, beer, and soft drinks
- ☐ White, brown, and powdered sugars
- ☐ Ground allspice, cinnamon, cloves, ginger, and nutmeg
- ☐ Baking soda and baking powder
- ☐ Seasonal fresh herbs
- ☐ Baking chocolate
- ☐ Semisweet chocolate morsels
- ☐ Assorted nuts
- ☐ Flaked coconut
- ☐ Sweetened condensed milk and evaporated milk
- ☐ Whipping cream
- ☐ Jams, jellies, and preserves
- ☐ Raisins, cranberries, and other fresh or dried fruits
- ☐ Canned pumpkin
- ☐ Frozen/refrigerated bread dough, biscuits, and croissants

Holiday Hotlines

Use these toll-free telephone numbers when you need answers to last-minute food questions.

-USDA Meat & Poultry Hotline:
1-800-535-4555
-FDA Center for Food Safety:
1-888-723-3366
-Butterball Turkey Talk Line:
1-800-288-8372
-The Reynolds Turkey Tips Hotline:
1-800-745-4000
-Betty Crocker (General Mills):
1-888-275-2388

DECEMBER *2012*

Sunday	Monday	Tuesday	Wednesday
2	3	4	5
9	10	11	12
16	17	18	19
23	24 Christmas Eve		
30	New Year's Eve 31	Christmas 25	26

Thursday	Friday	Saturday
		1
6	7	8
13	14	15
20	21	22
27	28	29

Don't let the hustle and bustle of the holidays stress you out when it comes to entertaining. Take advantage of these great convenience products at the grocery store to whip up a special dish to tote to the neighborhood get-together or office party.

- For an easy antipasto platter, arrange deli meats, cheeses, olives, pickled vegetables, assorted breadsticks and crackers, and prepared hummus onto a large platter. Garnish with fresh oregano and thyme.
- Add sliced grapes and toasted sliced almonds to deli-prepared chicken salad. Spoon into frozen, thawed phyllo cups for a great appetizer.
- Make a gourmet flatbread with pizza dough from the deli section of your grocery store. Pat it out onto a large jelly-roll pan, and bake at 450° for 10 minutes. Top with olive oil, chopped rosemary, fig preserves, walnuts, and goat cheese, and bake 5 to 10 minutes more until bread is crispy and golden.
- Make sweet-and-sour meatballs to feed a crowd. Place frozen meatballs in a large Dutch oven (no need to thaw). Pour 2 bottles of chili sauce and 2 jars of grape jelly into the pan, and stir gently to combine. Cover and cook over low heat 1 to 2 hours or until meatballs are hot and sauce is thickened.

Decorating PLANNER

List the finishing touches that you need to trim a picture-perfect house this season.

Decorative materials needed

from the yard ....
....

from around the house...
....

from the store...
....

other ....

Holiday decorations

for the table ....
....

for the door ....
....

for the mantel ....
....

for the staircase..
....

other ....

Reason for the Season

A time for giving and a time for cheer, Christmas is one of the most exciting times of the year. Though parties and presents are part of the fun, spending time with the ones you love as well as giving your time to those less fortunate will allow you to make memories and remember the real reason for the season. Try these ideas to make the most of your holiday.

• Contact your local United Way or Salvation Army to find out how your family can volunteer to help others in your community. Volunteering a couple of days or just one Saturday will make a difference in your area while allowing you to spend quality time together.

• Get your brood into the Christmas spirit even before Thanksgiving. Take your kids shopping to fill shoe boxes with toys, candy, and supplies for underprivileged children overseas. Your kids will have fun picking out the goodies to help another child have a brighter Christmas this year. Most collections for these shoe boxes take place in early November so research online early to find out information for drop-off locations in your area.

• Gather in the kitchen to prepare Christmas treats. Let your kids help with the baking as well as preparing boxes or bags for the treats. Older children can assist the little ones in delivering the goodies to neighbors and friends. Your kids will have fun sharing what they've made, and the recipients will appreciate your kindness.

• Ice skating is a fun activity that gets the family out of the house and allows you to get some exercise indoors while making memories together.

• Take some time for yourself and your family to slow down and relax with a festive flick. Gather your family on the couch to enjoy one of these Christmas classics. WIth a little hot chocolate and a cozy fire, this is sure to be one tradition the whole family will love.

Cozy Christmas Classics:

• *It's a Wonderful Life*
• *White Christmas*
• *Elf*

• *A Charlie Brown Christmas*
• *Miracle on 34th Street*
• *Home Alone*

Gifts for Everyone on YOUR LIST

While the holiday season is a time for parties, feasts, and general merrymaking, it's also a time for giving gifts that show you care. This Christmas, create elegant personalized gift baskets that are tailored to fit the interests of your family and friends.

• For the Gardener

For the friend who loves nothing more than putting her hands in the dirt, give a basket full of garden-ready essentials to use in that favorite outdoor space. Tuck a pair of brightly colored gardening gloves, some garden tools, seed packets, hand salve, and a gardening book into a watering can or lightweight planter. For a fragrant touch, add an herb-scented candle (such as rosemary or lavender) to bring the essence of the garden indoors.

• For the Hostess

The hostess is always providing for the needs of guests. Now you can take care of her for a change! Gather some beautiful household accessories to use at her next get-together such as recipe cards, mixing bowls, a set of drinking glasses, an oven mitt or apron with a fun print, and a coffee table book, and place them on a monogrammed serving tray. Include a pair of designer house slippers as a relaxing after-party treat.

• For the Sportsman

Not sure what to give the man who's crazy about sports? Whether he prefers fishing, hunting, or golf, center your gift around his favorite. For the golfer, place a lightweight polo shirt, a plush towel, a shoe brush, sunscreen, and some personalized golf balls in a handy wire basket that doubles as a golf ball holder. For the man who favors fishing, include sunglasses, a cap, artificial bait, and some gourmet snacks in a beverage tub for long days on the water.

• For the Food Enthusiast

Everyone has at least one friend who has amazing taste in food and wine, acquires the most delicious recipes, and always picks the best restaurants. For this person, you must simply indulge their refined palate. Bundle a box of decadent chocolates with a mix of cheeses, spiced nuts, personalized dinner plates, napkins, and a bottle of red wine. Tie them all up in a large woven basket that can later be used in the home or for a lovely picnic in the park.

• For the Southern Gentleman

Men of the South are distinctive and stylish, but they also enjoy the outdoors. For this man in your life, collect a few Southern-style necessities including a bow tie, initialed cuff links, a classic handkerchief, some barbecuing tools, a money clip, and a few bottles of locally brewed beer, and place in a sturdy leather tote bag or dresser caddy. Any or all of these gifts are certain to make the Southern man even more proud of his roots.

• For a Day at the Spa

After the busy holidays, what you really need is a day of luxurious relaxation. For those who can't make it to the spa right away, shower them with presents that bring the spa to their own home. Nothing says "relaxation" like the soothing fragrance of candles while soaking in a hot bath. For the ultimate spa package, combine lightly scented soy candles (such as gardenia or citrus), rich bubble bath, a headband, bath salts, and a terrycloth robe. Place these luxuries on a bamboo or metal bath caddy, and tie with natural jute or paper ribbon. For a little extra pampering, include coffee mugs, sachets of herbal tea, and a classic novel—sure to soothe body and mind.

Party PLANNER

Make sure your party plans stay on point with this time-saving menu chart.

guests	what they're bringing	serving pieces needed
....	☐ appetizer ☐ beverage ☐ bread ☐ main dish ☐ side dish ☐ dessert	....
....	☐ appetizer ☐ beverage ☐ bread ☐ main dish ☐ side dish ☐ dessert	....
....	☐ appetizer ☐ beverage ☐ bread ☐ main dish ☐ side dish ☐ dessert	....
....	☐ appetizer ☐ beverage ☐ bread ☐ main dish ☐ side dish ☐ dessert	....
....	☐ appetizer ☐ beverage ☐ bread ☐ main dish ☐ side dish ☐ dessert	....
....	☐ appetizer ☐ beverage ☐ bread ☐ main dish ☐ side dish ☐ dessert	....
....	☐ appetizer ☐ beverage ☐ bread ☐ main dish ☐ side dish ☐ dessert	....
....	☐ appetizer ☐ beverage ☐ bread ☐ main dish ☐ side dish ☐ dessert	....
....	☐ appetizer ☐ beverage ☐ bread ☐ main dish ☐ side dish ☐ dessert	....
....	☐ appetizer ☐ beverage ☐ bread ☐ main dish ☐ side dish ☐ dessert	....
....	☐ appetizer ☐ beverage ☐ bread ☐ main dish ☐ side dish ☐ dessert	....
....	☐ appetizer ☐ beverage ☐ bread ☐ main dish ☐ side dish ☐ dessert	....
....	☐ appetizer ☐ beverage ☐ bread ☐ main dish ☐ side dish ☐ dessert	....
....	☐ appetizer ☐ beverage ☐ bread ☐ main dish ☐ side dish ☐ dessert	....
....	☐ appetizer ☐ beverage ☐ bread ☐ main dish ☐ side dish ☐ dessert	....
....	☐ appetizer ☐ beverage ☐ bread ☐ main dish ☐ side dish ☐ dessert	....
....	☐ appetizer ☐ beverage ☐ bread ☐ main dish ☐ side dish ☐ dessert	....

Party Guest List

Pantry List

Party To-Do List

Christmas Dinner PLANNER

You and your holiday celebration will stay organized with the menu, to-do list, and guest list in our handy meal planner.

Menu Ideas

....
....
....
....
....
....
....

Dinner To-Do List

....
....
....
....
....
....
....

Christmas Dinner Guest List

....
....
....
....
....
....
....
....
....

Mix-and-Match MENUS

Menus below are based on recipes in the book.

CHRISTMAS OPEN HOUSE

Bacon-Wrapped Blue Cheese Dates (page 123)

Red or Green Pepper Jelly (1 jar) with a round of Brie (page 166)

Barbecued Pork Tartlets with Slaw Topping (page 122)

Greek Meatballs with Tzatziki Sauce (page 125)

Cranberry Salsa (page 121)

Parmesan-Crusted Crab Cake Bites with Chive Aïoli (page 27)

Butterscotch-Pecan Tassies (page 104)

Serves 10 to 12

NEW YEAR'S EVE DESSERT PARTY

Sparkling Blood Orange Cocktail (2x) (page 26)

Gingersnap-Meyer Lemon Meringue Tart (page 145)

Baklava Cheesecake (page 143)

Buckeye Brownie Cups (page 40)

White Chocolate-Peppermint Mousse Pie (page 107)

Serves 12

BREAKFAST FOR DINNER

Andouille and Spinach Pie (page 98) or

Ham and Cheese Croissant Strata (page 96)

Gouda-Pancetta Grits Casserole (page 98)

mixed fruit salad

Serves 6 to 8

SWANKY SOIRÉE

Garlic-Herb Rib Roast (page 128)

Bacon-Caramelized Onion-Spinach Bake (page 135)

Seared Radicchio with Balsamic Glaze (page 139)

Horseradish-Spiked Cauliflower Gratin (page 137)

Double-Chocolate Chess Pie (page 106)

Serves 8

COZY WEEKNIGHT SUPPER

Chicken-Gouda Tetrazzini (page 129)

Sweet and Savory Roasted Green Beans (page 30)

Rosemary-Gruyère Buns (page 20)

Mini Apple-Cranberry Pies (page 108)

Serves 4

SLUMBER PARTY

Lemony Feta Dip with Oven-Roasted Tomatoes (page 121)

The Farmer's Pizza (page 111)

Carne Lover's Pizza (page 114)

Asian Pear and Hazelnut Salad (page 21)

Brown Sugar-Ginger Cookie Trifle (page 145)

Serves 8

Gifts AND *Greetings*

Keep up with relatives' sizes, jot down gift ideas, and record purchases in this convenient chart. Also use it to add to your ever-growing Christmas card list.

Gift List and Size Charts

name /sizes	gift purchased/made	sent/delivered

name ....

jeans_____ shirt_____ sweater_____ jacket_____ shoes_____ belt_____

blouse_____ skirt_____ slacks_____ dress_____ suit_____ coat_____

pajamas_____ robe_____ hat_____ gloves_____ ring_____

name ....

jeans_____ shirt_____ sweater_____ jacket_____ shoes_____ belt_____

blouse_____ skirt_____ slacks_____ dress_____ suit_____ coat_____

pajamas_____ robe_____ hat_____ gloves_____ ring_____

name ....

jeans_____ shirt_____ sweater_____ jacket_____ shoes_____ belt_____

blouse_____ skirt_____ slacks_____ dress_____ suit_____ coat_____

pajamas_____ robe_____ hat_____ gloves_____ ring_____

name ....

jeans_____ shirt_____ sweater_____ jacket_____ shoes_____ belt_____

blouse_____ skirt_____ slacks_____ dress_____ suit_____ coat_____

pajamas_____ robe_____ hat_____ gloves_____ ring_____

name ....

jeans_____ shirt_____ sweater_____ jacket_____ shoes_____ belt_____

blouse_____ skirt_____ slacks_____ dress_____ suit_____ coat_____

pajamas_____ robe_____ hat_____ gloves_____ ring_____

name ....

jeans_____ shirt_____ sweater_____ jacket_____ shoes_____ belt_____

blouse_____ skirt_____ slacks_____ dress_____ suit_____ coat_____

pajamas_____ robe_____ hat_____ gloves_____ ring_____

name ....

jeans_____ shirt_____ sweater_____ jacket_____ shoes_____ belt_____

blouse_____ skirt_____ slacks_____ dress_____ suit_____ coat_____

pajamas_____ robe_____ hat_____ gloves_____ ring_____

Christmas Card List

name	address	sent/delivered

HOLIDAY *Memories*

Cherish your holiday for years to come with handwritten recollections of this season's memorable moments.

Treasured Traditions

Keep track of your family's favorite holiday customs and pastimes on these lines.

....

....

....

....

....

....

....

....

....

....

....

....

....

Special Holiday Activities

What holiday events do you look forward to year after year? Write them down here.

....

....

....

....

....

....

....

....

Holiday Visits and Visitors

Keep a list of this year's holiday visitors. Jot down friend
and family news as well.

....
....
....
....
....
....
....
....
....
....
....
....
....
....
....
....
....
....
....
....
....
....
....
....
....
....

This Year's Favorite Recipes

Appetizers and Beverages ....
....
....
....
....
....

Entrées ....
....
....
....

Sides and Salads ....
....
....
....
....

Cookies and Candies ....
....
....
....
....

Desserts ....
....
....
....
....

Holiday Wrap-up

Use this checklist to record thank-you notes sent for holiday gifts and hospitality.

name	gift and/or event	note sent
		☐
		☐
		☐
		☐
		☐
		☐
		☐
		☐
		☐
		☐
		☐
		☐
		☐

Notes for Next Year

Write down your ideas for Christmas 2013 in the lines below.